Broadman Church Manual

BROADMAN CHURCH MANUAL

■

Howard B. Foshee

BROADMAN PRESS · Nashville, Tennessee

Dedication

To past and present staff members
of the Church Administration Department,
Sunday School Board of the Southern
Baptist Convention, who have labored so
diligently in developing concepts and
approaches for more effective church
administration, many of which appear
in this book.

ISBN: 0–8054–2525-x
4225–25

Library of Congress Catalog Card Number: 72–94629
Dewey Decimal Classification Number: 262
Printed in the United States of America

CONTENTS

1. CHURCH
Nature, Functions, Membership

Nature

The nature of the church is one of divine origin, divine leadership, and divine purpose.

1. *Divine Origin*

Christ instituted the church as a vital part of God's divine plan for man. The origin of the church was in and through Christ.

God has revealed himself in many ways and many times throughout the centuries. God revealed himself through Abraham. The nation Israel was an instrument of God's revelation. God sent Christ, his Son, to proclaim the gospel of salvation. Christ came proclaiming "I am the way, the truth, and the life: no man cometh unto the Father, but by me" (John 14:6).

Christ established his church to carry forward his message of salvation after his early ministry was completed. Paul wrote of Christ: "And hath put all things under his feet, and gave him to be the head over all things to the church, which is his body, the fulness of him that filleth all in all" (Eph. 1:22–23).

Christ entrusted his church to redeemed persons to forward God's plan on earth. "And I say also unto thee, That thou art Peter, and upon this rock I will build my church; and the gates of hell shall not prevail against it" (Matt. 16:18). Christians today must bear the awesome responsibility for faithful service to the church.

The foundation of the church is Christ. He is its chief cornerstone. His church is not an institution made by the hands of man. As a spiritual organism, the church is a living body that received its life from God, the divine source of all life. Members of the church are redeemed persons who are new persons in Christ. "Therefore if any man be in Christ, he is a new creature: old things are passed away; behold, all things are become new" (2 Cor. 5:17).

The word "church" comes from the Greek word *ekklesia,* which means "the called out." As "called out" persons, redeemed in Christ, Christians gather as the church in fellowship and worship. They then go out into the world to proclaim the gospel message to the world.

Most of the times when *ekklesia* appears in the New Testament, the word refers to a local congregation. There is adequate reference to the total body of Christians, however, to assure that *ekklesia* also refers to all redeemed persons in Christ.

2. *Divine Leadership*

As head of the church, Christ provides continuing leadership. The church is his body.

Christ said that he purchased the church with his own blood. He will not let it be overcome. "Take heed therefore unto yourselves, and to all the flock, over the which the Holy Ghost hath made you overseers, to feed the church of God, which he hath purchased with his own blood" (Acts 20:28).

Forces of evil bombard the church, but Christ, the divine leader, cannot be subdued. Evil may sometimes prevail for a season in the world. Satan may win an occasional battle. But the war against evil will be won by Christians who witness alongside fellow believers.

Christ, as leader of the church, has all power (authority). "And Jesus came and spake unto them, saying, All power is given unto me in heaven and in earth" (Matt. 28:18). Christians should rejoice in the knowledge that the church is led by Christ, the possessor of all power.

3. *Divine Purpose*

Christ established the church to carry out his divine purpose. The purpose of Christ and the purpose of his church are identical.

Christians, as baptized believers, are to gather as the church for spiritual fellowship, encouragement, training, and worship of God. Christians are then to go out as the living body of Christ, the church, to dwell in the world as proclaimers of Christ's message of redemption.

Christians have their marching orders. Christ, their leader, commanded: "Go ye therefore, and teach all nations, baptizing them in the name of the Father, and of the Son, and of the Holy Ghost: Teaching them to observe all things whatsoever I have commanded you:

and, lo, I am with you alway, even unto the end of the
world" (Matt. 28:19–20).

Members of the church are to carry out their purpose in a spirit of love. God is love and his work must
be permeated with love. He gave his followers a commandment regarding their way of life. "A new commandment I give unto you, That ye love one another.
. . . By this shall all men know that ye are my disciples,
if ye have love one to another" (John 13:34–35).

Church Functions

A church is a spiritual organism. As a living organism the church has basic spiritual functions to perform
that are essential to its life. As the human body cannot
continue to live if basic bodily functions cease, neither
can the body of Christ (church) continue if its basic
functions cease.

What are these basic functions that are so essential
to the life and work of a church? They are: to worship,
to proclaim, to educate, and to minister.

1. *To Worship*

To worship is to become aware of the holy presence
of God and to follow God's leadership in love. Baptists
believe in a personal God who loves and desires fellowship with man. Worship is man's adoration and
confession to God and God's communion with man.
Worship is man's link with God in his search for truth.
"But the hour cometh, and now is, when the true
worshippers shall worship the Father in spirit and in
truth: for the Father seeketh such to worship him. God

is Spirit: and they that worship him must worship him in spirit and in truth" (John 4:23–24).

Man responds to God through worship and dedicates himself to serve God. Worship is not complete until man serves God as a result of their two-way communication. The desire of the Christian is that of the psalmist: "O come, let us worship and bow down: let us kneel before the Lord our maker" (Ps. 95:6).

2. *To Proclaim*

To proclaim is to provide a witness for the gospel message of Jesus Christ who came to provide salvation for man. The church must place high priority on its proclamation function. A church that does not proclaim God's message of salvation has lost its heart. Christ commanded: "Go ye therefore, and teach all nations, baptizing them in the name of the Father, and of the Son, and of the Holy Ghost: Teaching them to observe all things whatsoever I have commanded you: and lo, I am with you alway, even unto the end of the world" (Matt. 28:19–20).

The gospel must be proclaimed to both believers and unbelievers. The message of salvation provides spiritual nourishment to the Christian. To the unbeliever the gospel opens up a new life in Christ when accepted in faith.

Churches should use a variety of methods in proclaiming God's message. The gospel can be proclaimed through such means as preaching, personal witness, music, and Bible teaching.

3. *To Educate*

"To educate is to lead persons to the knowledge and acceptance of Jesus Christ as Saviour and Lord, to teach and train the church's constituency to perform the functions of their church, and to help them develop toward full Christian maturity" (from *A Church Organized and Functioning* by W. L. Howse and W. O. Thomason).

A church should be a fellowship of learners. Christ set the example. "Jesus increased in wisdom and stature, and in favour with God and man" (Luke 2:52). Learning opportunities are essential because persons need to be able to increase their knowledge and understanding of spiritual matters. Each Christian should seek out learning opportunities that are provided in order to become more like Christ. Skills in Christian living should be taught to equip members for daily living. A growing Christian is a learner who exercises the personal discipline required to grow in knowledge and Christlikeness.

Christ is the source of spiritual wisdom and Christians need to learn of him "that their hearts might be comforted, being knit together in love, and unto all riches of the full assurance of understanding, to the acknowledgement of the mystery of God, and of the Father, and of Christ; in whom are hid all the treasures of wisdom and knowledge" (Col. 2:2–3).

4. *To Minister*

To minister is to respond to man's needs in love so that Christ Jesus can be magnified.

A ministering church seeks to serve man in Christ's name. Ministering to the needs of man was taught by Christ. During his early ministry Jesus healed the sick, raised the dead, and comforted the brokenhearted. Christ was concerned for the total needs of man as he reached out with God's message of salvation. "Beloved, let us love one another: for love is of God; and every one that loveth is born of God, and knoweth God" (1 John 4:7).

Ministering in Christ's name is done without thought of personal return. A Christian offers himself and his resources because God's love fills him. He reaches out in love to Christian and non-Christian.

Ministering is a vital function of a church that grows out of God's love for man. The Christian should demonstrate his love. Jesus taught: "A new commandment I give unto you, that ye love one another; as I have loved you, that ye also love one another. By this shall all men know that ye are my disciples, if ye have love one to another" (John 13:34–35).

Church Membership

The church was established by Christ as a part of God's divine plan. As church members, Christians have gathered through the centuries for corporate worship, fellowship, nurture, and service. Churches serve as spiritual oases for the weary pilgrim who seeks fellowship with God and fellow believers. Churches serve as mighty mission stations as well as dedicated mission forces that go forth as Christian soldiers to spread the gospel.

Church membership provides redeemed persons an opportunity for binding together with fellow Christians to worship and glorify God. As members of Christ's body, Christians find spiritual strength and direction through fellowship with other believers.

As a member of a church, an individual must discipline himself to live a life in Christ. He must participate in both remedial and preventive discipline to protect the spiritual nature of the church. He must also participate constructively in making congregational decisions that influence the life and work of the church.

1. *Qualifications*

A church member must be a redeemed person who has confessed his sins and has accepted Christ as Savior and Lord of his life. He must be one who has opened his life for examination and has publicly declared that he desires to invest his life in covenant relationship with other Christians. He has been baptized as a symbol of his death and burial to sin and of his resurrection to a new life in Christ.

2. *Methods of Accepting Members*

There are three methods of accepting members: profession of faith, transfer of church membership, and statement of baptism.

(1) *Profession of faith (by baptism).*—A person may unite with a Baptist church by profession of faith in Christ as Savior and Lord, followed by baptism. A

profession of faith is usually made by an individual at the conclusion of a church worship service. By presenting himself for membership in a church, a person affirms that he desires to become a participant in the fellowship of believers in Christ.

(2) *Transfer of church membership (by letter).*—An individual may join a Baptist church by transfer of church membership from another Baptist church. This method of membership transfer is popularly called "by letter." As a person presents himself to a new church "by letter," he requests that he be received upon the later receipt of a letter acknowledging his membership in another Baptist church. When his letter of recommendation is finally received, stating that he is a baptized believer in good standing in his church, he is then recognized as a member of his new church.

In effect, a church affirms its appreciation of a person when he publicly requests membership in a new church. He does not become an actual member until proof of his membership has been received.

(3) *Statement of baptism.*—If for some reason an individual's church record has been lost, his church has been disbanded, or he may have joined a church of another denomination, a person may request that he be received into the fellowship of a church by stating that he has previously accepted Christ as Lord and Savior and has been baptized. If the church votes to receive the person upon his statement, the church usually does not require baptism in view of his earlier baptism in a Baptist church.

3. *Types of Church Membership*

Resident membership indicates that a person lives within a geographical territory that allows him to attend his church. The member may not attend, but the distance from his residence to his church does not prevent his attendance.

Nonresident membership acknowledges that a member lives outside the geographical location of his church and is therefore unable to attend regularly. Churches should encourage their members who have moved away to join a Baptist church in their community.

Watchcare represents a short-term relationship one may have with a church. Students or military persons who will be able to attend only a few months sometimes request that they be received by watchcare. While attending a church under watchcare, a person usually does not have voting privileges.

4. *Responsibilities of Church Members*

A church that operates under congregational polity places heavy responsibility on individual members. As individual members participate in the corporate activities of a church, they must make major decisions that influence the life and work of the church. The congregation, as the body of Christ, has significant decisions to make and unique work to perform. What are the responsibilities of church members? What work must the congregation perform? What decisions must be made by the church members?

The following responsibilities delineate some of the work that is required of the congregation.

1. *Govern the church's life and work under the lordship of Christ.*—Each member of the congregation must accept responsibility for participating in the decision-making processes that govern the life and work of the church. These decisions should be made under the leadership of the Lord. Congregational polity holds forth lofty leadership precepts that should elicit the finest qualities from persons. Governing a church requires more from members than voting routinely on issues presented in business session. Each member of the church should prayerfully seek the leadership of the Lord in matters relating to the work of the church. A major task of the congregation must always be to govern itself under the leadership of the Lord.

2. *Participate in the corporate life and work of the fellowship.*—One of the noblest expressions of individual freedom is the choice of participation with other persons in an endeavor of mutual concern. An important aspect of work of each congregation is to participate collectively in being a Christian fellowship that functions in worship, witness, education, ministry, and application. Personal involvement brings spiritual growth as the congregational members participate in the basic functions of the church.

Major bodily systems are essential to human life. Without respiration and circulation, life cannot continue for an individual. Likewise, a church has basic functions that are essential to its existence as a spiritual organism. When a church ceases to worship

or witness, for example, it ceases to be the body of
Christ. Christians, bonded together as the body of
Christ, have responsibility for participating collec-
tively in the functions of the church.

3. *Take part in cooperative work with other churches.*—A
bond of Christian fellowship should exist between all
persons who know the Lord as Savior. A basic responsibility of the congregation is to decide when to join
cooperatively with other churches of like faith in projects that are of mutual concern. Responsibility for
maintaining healthy relationships is an ongoing task
of the congregation.

Mutual fulfilment results when Baptist churches fellowship with one another in associations and/or conventions. Functioning as a group, churches can participate in mission activities, for example, that far
excel their own capacity to minister in love.

Members of a congregation have responsibility for
establishing cooperative relations and for mutually
supporting work with other churches of similar faith
and order.

4. *Establish and take part in relationships with appropriate
publics.*—A basic task of the congregation is to relate
to the various publics with which it has significant
contact. Jesus commanded that Christians go into all
the world proclaiming the gospel. He also reminded
Christians that a light should not be hidden under a
bushel.

A church, likewise, needs to relate appropriately to
its publics outside the membership. The message of
Christ must be proclaimed to every person and groups

of persons. A church should relate in mission action where needs exist. Public officials need to be commended for actions. Expression of concern should be voiced by the church when moral deterioration is evident.

Church members have responsibility for seeing that proper relations are established and maintained with various publics that touch the life and work of the church. These relationships are for the purpose of helping the church achieve its objectives.

5. *Make resources available for the work of the church.*— Resources must be provided and allocated by the congregation according to priority. Resources of various kinds are required by a church. Christians grow as stewards when efforts are directed by the church for securing resources primarily from its own members. Resources such as finances, buildings, and personnel are essential for carrying out the work of the church.

Church members must make decisions regarding the budget, such as how much it will be and how it will be spent. In addition, individual members must share their finances to support the church financial needs. Christians grow in spiritual stature when they give sacrificially of their financial resources.

Church members must also approve the selection of all church leaders. All church leaders must be elected by the congregation.

6. *Train persons in the skills for Christian living.*—The congregation has responsibility for providing learning opportunities to help persons acquire skills for Christian living. The Bible should be a primary resource for

such training. Christians should seek to grow daily in spiritual stature. Growth comes by activities such as personal devotional study and involvement in matters of spiritual service. Opportunities need to be provided by the church for its members to strengthen their faith through Bible study, training, and mission action.

7. *Train members in the meaning of church membership.*— Churches must train members to carry out the work of the church. The spiritual nature of the church requires persons of deep spiritual commitment. One of the basic tasks of the church is to equip its members to minister effectively. Persons need training in personal witnessing. Bible knowledge should be high on any priority list for church leaders. Skill in music and mission action is desirable. Church members need knowledge of Christian theology, Christian ethics, and Christian history. Information should also be shared about the total work of the church and denomination.

The congregation must accept final responsibility for seeing that a church is so organized as to provide the training necessary to get its work accomplished.

8. *Proclaim the gospel to all persons.*—When a church ceases to proclaim the gospel to believers and unbelievers, it fails to carry out one of the foundations for its existence. Church members must share their Christian experiences with every person they contact. The gospel of Jesus Christ must be declared and demonstrated. Believers need to be constantly encouraged with the heartwarming message of Christ. Unbelievers must be reached.

A congregation has responsibility for taking action

to see that the message of Christ is proclaimed in every appropriate manner.

9. *Reach persons for Christ and church membership.* —Making disciples is at the center of the church's work. One of the basic responsibilities of the church, therefore, is to reach people for Christ and church membership. Congregation members must see that adequate resources are allocated to activities for reaching persons for Christ. Organizations should be established and mobilized to reach people.

The congregation must establish and maintain guidelines by which regenerate persons will be admitted into the fellowship. Decisions must also be made regarding the dismissal of members.

2. CHURCH POLITY AND GOVERNMENT
Meaning and Types

Acts 6 offers the first account of a church establishing procedures by which a congregation handled a fellowship problem. Members of the Jerusalem church had sought to share their faith and their possessions with one another. Problems of personal relationship developed when the Greek-speaking widows complained that they were being treated unfairly.

The apostles suggested to their fellow believers that seven qualified persons be appointed by the church to confront the problem.

The seven apparently were highly successful. The writer of Acts says: "And the word of God increased; and the number of the disciples multiplied in Jerusalem greatly; and a great company of the priests were obedient to the faith" (Acts 6:7).

Each church needs some plan of government by which it will guide and direct its work. Government establishes the foundation on which church members can implement their work with harmony and dispatch. Government and polity are family members. Both government and polity are extremely important in the life and work of a church.

Polity defines the place of authority and power. Polity speaks to the basic character of decision-making

and final appeal. Government, on the other hand, provides methods by which principles of polity can be
implemented.

Types of Church Polity

There are five basic types of polity exercised by
religious groups today in America. The four basic
polity types as seen in American churches are congregational, episcopal, monarchial, and presbyterian.
The fifth basic polity is Erastian. Erastian polity, not
generally found in America, calls for the church to be
ruled by state or civil authority.

1. *Congregational*

Baptists follow a congregational polity in which individual members have equal authority under the
leadership of the Holy Spirit. Belief in the priesthood
of the believer is a basic foundation that has greatly
influenced Baptists in their close adherence to congregational polity.

Churches that follow congregational polity govern
themselves. The church membership, under the leadership of the Holy Spirit, is the ruling body. The congregation is not an organic part of any clerical hierarchy. Its decisions.are final and cannot be overruled
by any outside authority.

Persons participating in congregational decisions
bear a heavy responsibility. Each person is, of course,
free to express his personal opinions during discussions. But each member should remember that he is
to seek his own understanding in light of the Holy

Spirit's leadership. Opinions expressed in congregational business meetings should be expressions
bathed in the spirit of patience and Christian love.
Congregational church polity seeks to find the best
answer in light of Christ's will.

Church members have equal rights and authority.
Church leaders elected by the church receive instruction regarding their work from the congregation.
They report back to the congregation. Following open
discussion of church matters, each church member has
the right to vote his own conviction.

Churches following true congregational polity do
not send *delegates* to association, state Baptist convention, or Southern Baptist Convention meetings. Neither does a church hold formal membership in these
equally autonomous groups. Church members are appointed by the church to attend meetings of these
separate groups. These *messengers* vote as individuals
and not as delegates representing the church.

2. *Episcopal*

Churches that follow episcopal polity believe that
authority should rest with a few persons at the top of
a clerical hierarchy. A bishop has final administrative
authority over a group of churches which are generally
located in a geographical territory.

A local church is administered by vestrymen, who
act as an official board. Although these and other laymen participate in some decisions, certain areas of
work are handled exclusively by the clergy. Examples
of these matters are questions related to discipline,

doctrinal statements, and clerical ordination.

The Methodist and Episcopal churches follow variations of episcopal polity. There are descending levels of authority housed in the clergy of the Episcopal Church. The highest authority is vested in the House of Bishops, which is composed of all the bishops in the United States. In the Methodist Church. the layman plays a larger role than in the Episcopal Church. Members of the General Conference, composed of delegates from the Annual Conference throughout several territories, make the major decisions regarding matters of significant nature.

There is at present a growing involvement of laymen in both the Episcopal and Methodist churches.

3. *Monarchial*

Monarchial polity has characteristics similar to episcopal polity. The highest legislative and judicial decisions are made by high-ranking clergy who have been appointed as bishops. The chief distinctive of monarchial polity over episcopal polity is that one bishop has been selected to have final authority over the other bishops. The Roman Catholic Church, which is ruled by the pope, is an example of monarchial polity. The pope is chosen to determine decisions of highest rank.

Power and authority flow from the pope in descending order to bishops and priests. In monarchial polity, decisions are made at high levels and passed downward. There is a minimum of lay participation in the affairs of a hierarchial government founded on monarchial polity. Decrees regarding such things as doctrines and worship rituals are decided by the clergy and passed down to the laity.

In recent years the lay members of the Roman Catholic Church in the United States have shown evidence of securing more voice in the affairs of their church.

4. *Presbyterian*

Presbyterian polity is a representative type of polity. Each church elects elders (presbyters) who are delegated authority. Unlike monarchial polity no one elder has authority above other elders. In addition to elders, Presbyterian churches also elect deacons. Deacons serve primarily in the implementation of administrative matters.

Churches are governed by their elected elders. The pastor is not a member of the church but rather is a member of the presbytery of which the church is a member. Presbyteries are grouped together in a geographical territory. The membership of a presbytery is composed of the various churches in a presbytery. The highest legislative and judicial body is the General Assembly, which is composed of members of the presbyteries.

Appeals for decisions flow upward, and decisions on appeals flow downward in presbyterian polity.

Laymen have considerable involvement in presbyterian polity. They are elected to participate as representatives in the various levels in presbyterian hierarchy.

3. CHURCH COVENANT
How to Develop Your Own

Covenants are to be experienced. They are not to be followed slavishly as a legal document or to be used as an inflexible set of rules that are displayed on the inside cover of the church hymnal. Each church needs to develop its own covenant statement that accurately describes the commitment to God and fellow Christians that the church members have affirmed.

A church covenant statement should evolve from the crucible of Christian experience. This experience of commitment to God and fellow believers should then be written as a reminder and a guide.

Both the Old Testament and the New Testament are rich in examples of covenant relationships. God created a community of covenant people. He was their God and they were his people. They were bound together by a common mission. They were molded together by a pervading faith in God and a fellowship with one another. Common heritage, goals, and fellowship bound them as one.

Jesus came proclaiming a new covenant. He provided the Lord's Supper, an occasion when Christian commitment could again be celebrated and fellowship in Christ could be experienced. "This cup is the new testament [covenant] in my blood: this do ye, as oft

21

as ye drink it, in remembrance of me" (1 Cor. 11:25).

As Christians experience a covenant relationship in Christ, they grow in their concern for persons without Christ. They open themselves in honesty to one another to express their deepest inward thoughts. Openness, forgiveness, and compassion bind these Christians together.

A covenant relationship, however, does not occur spontaneously. Just because church members meet together for worship does not insure that they will experience the warmth of spiritual fellowship *(koinonia)*. They must share their lives in Christ. Each must provide mutual support for others who are also on a spiritual pilgrimage. As they pray, sing, share their faith, open their hearts in confession, and express genuine concern for others, they become a people of Christian covenant. These experiences of commitment to God and fellow Christians lead to the deep rewards of covenant.

Guidelines for Developing a Church Covenant

Every church needs its own covenant statement that expresses the covenant relationship that exists within that church. The use of a church covenant statement that has been prepared by another church is not adequate. A church covenant is a personal commitment that must be developed by the church members who have experienced a revitalizing relationship with God in Christ and with fellow Christians.

There are several popular statements of church

covenants that have been used widely by churches. For a covenant statement to be meaningful to a congregation, it should be developed prayerfully through group processes that involve as many of the church members as possible.

Many churches have found the following process helpful in developing their own covenant statement.

1. *Select a Special Committee*

The committee should be elected by the church. It should be a special committee that will be dismissed after the work has been completed. Its membership should be composed of persons whose lives demonstrate a vital relationship with Christ and with their fellow Christians.

The church covenant committee should involve as many church members as possible in the development of the church covenant statement. The committee coordinates the development of a church covenant rather than doing all the preparation alone. A covenant is not a legal document. It is an expression of commitment made between persons who love God and each other.

2. *Study Available Church Covenants*

A review of other church covenants will help the committee. Study various covenants to examine their content and style. Talk with persons who may have participated in the development of a church covenant statement.

3. *Involve Church Members in Developing the Covenant*

Members of the committee should meet with various groups in the church to seek their help. Deacons, Sunday School classes, training groups, missionary groups, committees, and councils should be given opportunity to express their views as to what should be included in the covenant. Members of the covenant committee should listen carefully and record the concerns expressed.

All persons participating in these input sessions should understand that their views are for resource and may not be used verbatim in the final covenant.

The pastor may choose to preach a series of sermons on the covenant relationship that should exist among fellow Christians. These sermons can be helpful if preached prior to group discussions about what the covenant should contain. Use every means possible to communicate to church members the purpose, value, and process being used in the development of the church covenant.

4. *Prepare Draft of Church Covenant*

After collecting as much information as possible from church members, the covenant committee should then develop the first draft of a proposed covenant statement. Do not rush. Most committees take several weeks to complete this work.

5. *Secure Evaluation of the Proposed Covenant Draft*

Seek evaluation from the various persons and groups who have provided input. If the pastor and church staff members have not participated in the committee work, they should be given opportunity to provide evaluation. Their insights can be helpful.

Mail copies of the covenant to all church members requesting that they return their evaluations by a certain date.

Use every appropriate method to get response from as many church members as possible.

6. *Prepare Final Draft of Covenant for Church Action*

The committee should review all proposed evaluations and then prepare the final draft for recommendation to the church. The covenant should again be made available to every church member for review and evaluation. The committee should use these evaluations to strengthen the covenant.

Church approval of the church covenant should be at a time when a maximum number of members can be present to vote.

7. *Use the Church Covenant*

After approval by the church, the covenant should be printed and distributed. Consider placing the covenant on the inside covers of the church hymnals. Plan creative ways to use the covenant in worship services so that members may be reminded regularly of their commitment to God and to one another.

Sample Church Covenant 1

The oldest and most widely used covenant by Baptist churches was first developed by the New Hampshire Baptist Convention in conjunction with a confession of faith adopted in 1833. The covenant was first published in pamphlet form in 1833.

Subsequently, the covenant was revised on numerous occasions and appeared in various publications. Some of the revised covenant statements appeared in *Baptist Church Manual* by J. Newton Brown, 1855; *Baptist Church Directory* by Edward T. Hiscox, 1859; *Church Manual* by J. M. Pendleton, 1867. The manual by Pendleton brought wide usage of the covenant by Baptist churches.

Growing out of a recommendation at the 1970 Southern Baptist Convention to study the possible revision of the covenant appearing in the *Baptist Hymnal* and elsewhere, the following phrase was added, "to use our influence to combat the use of drugs and the spread of pornography," to the already existing phrase, "to abstain from the sale and use of intoxicating drinks as a beverage."

The following three sample church covenants appear in the booklet by James E. Fitch entitled *Developing a Church Covenant,* published by the Sunday School Board, and are used here by permission.

CHURCH COVENANT 1

Having been led, as we believe, by the Spirit of God, to receive the Lord Jesus Christ as our Saviour,

And on the profession of our faith, having been baptized in the name of the Father, and of the Son, and of the Holy Ghost,

We do now, in the presence of God, angels, and this

assembly, most solemnly and joyfully enter into covenant with one another, as one body in Christ.

We engage, therefore, by the aid of the Holy Spirit, to walk together in Christian love; to strive for the advancement of this church, in knowledge, holiness, and comfort;

To promote its prosperity and spirituality; to sustain its worship, ordinances, discipline, and doctrines;

To contribute cheerfully and regularly to the support of the ministry, the expenses of the church, the relief of the poor, and the spread of the gospel through all nations.

We also engage to maintain family and secret devotions; to religiously educate our children; to seek the salvation of our kindred and acquaintances;

To walk circumspectly in the world; to be just in our dealings, faithful in our engagements, and exemplary in our deportment;

To avoid all tattling, backbiting, and excessive anger;

To abstain from the sale and use of intoxicating drinks as a beverage; to use our influence to combat the abuse of drugs and the spread of pornography; and to be zealous in our efforts to advance the kingdom of our Saviour.

We further engage to watch over one another in brotherly love;

To remember one another in prayer; to aid one another in sickness and distress; to cultivate Christian sympathy in feeling and courtesy in speech;

To be slow to take offense, but always ready for

reconciliation, and mindful of the rules of our Saviour to secure it without delay.

We moreover engage that when we remove from this place we will, as soon as possible, unite with some other church, where we can carry out the spirit of this covenant and the principles of God's Word.

Sample Church Covenant 2

Covenant 2 is based on an earlier covenant form, which was adopted in 1846 by the Maine Baptist Convention. *The Church Member's Manual* by William Crowell included the covenant in 1847. The statement was used in many Baptist churches.

Again in 1904 *The Church Covenant Idea* by Champlin Burrage published the covenant. Churches used the covenant or revisions of it for many years.

Sample Covenant 2, a revision of the Maine Baptist Convention Covenant, was developed in the late 1800's by the Immanuel Baptist Church, Nashville, Tennessee. In 1967, the church revised the covenant statement as it now appears below.

CHURCH COVENANT 2

Since we have committed ourselves to Jesus Christ and have experienced the acceptance, forgiveness, and redemption of God our Father, we covenant together as members of this church that with God's help through the guiding presence of his Spirit:

We will walk together in brotherly love.

We will show loving care for one another and encourage, counsel and admonish one another.

We will assemble faithfully for worship and fellowship, and will pray earnestly for others as well as for
ourselves.

We will endeavor to bring up those under our care
"in the nurture and admonition of the Lord."

We will seek, by Christian example and personal
effort, to win others to Christ and to encourage their
growth toward Christian maturity.

We will share one another's joys and endeavor to
bear one another's burdens and sorrows.

We will oppose all conduct which compromises our
Christian faith and will uphold high standards of
Christian morality.

We will prove the reality of our conversion by living
godly, fruitful lives.

We will maintain a faithful ministry of worship, witness, education, fellowship, and service.

We will be faithful stewards of our resources and
abilities in sharing the gospel with people of all nations.

As a result of this covenant relationship, we will seek
earnestly to live to the glory of God who brought us
out of darkness into his marvelous light.

Sample Church Covenant 3

Covenant 3, prepared by James E. Fitch in 1970, is
written in a contemporary style. This covenant is written in a highly personal style and approaches relationships of church members from different perspectives.
Members are asked to feel an awareness of personal
relationship and commitment to God as well as an

awareness of brotherhood with other Christian believers.

CHURCH COVENANT 3

We covenant with God our Father:

We accept, O Lord, your forgiveness for the sins we have committed, and pray that you will stop their harmful effects; we covenant with you, to be forgiving persons.

We thank you, O Lord, for touching our hearts and lives with your healing; we covenant with you, to be healers to others.

We thank you, our Father, for making us aware of your presence; we covenant with you, to watch for, wait upon, and depend on your help daily in our lives.

We thank you, O Lord, for making us aware of who we are, and for helping us to understand others; we covenant with you, to be understanding persons.

We thank you, O Lord, for accepting us as persons, when we are so far from being holy and righteous; we covenant with you, to be persons who accept others even when they do not measure up to our standards.

We thank you, O Lord, for being interested in our lives; we covenant with you, to let your son Jesus be our Lord.

We recognize, O Lord, the steadfastness of your faithfulness to us; we return that commitment and dedicate our lives to you and your service.

We thank you, O Lord, for breaking some of the sinful bonds on our lives; we covenant with you to be

Christian toward those who are not experiencing this freedom.

We thank you, O Lord, for loving us when we do not deserve your love; we covenant with you, to love others as you have loved us.

We covenant with one another:

Because God has accepted me, I accept you, my brethren, into my life and into my care. I covenant to accept you as you are, and hope that we can grow together to be mature children of God.

Because I have experienced the forgiveness of God in my life, I covenant with you, as a brother in Christ, to forgive you, even when I feel the pain you may cause me.

Because I know God's help and support in my life, I covenant, my brethren, to support you to the best of my abilities, in times of your grief, stress, and sickness.

Because we are members of Christ's body, the church, I covenant with you to share life and service with you, with all of its joys and sorrows. I covenant to be concerned about you and your family. I promise to defend you as brethren from those who would deny you their love and respect. I covenant to be honest with you, even when it may be painful to us both.

I covenant to respond when you try to help me. I promise to trust that you act from a concern for me.

I covenant with you, that henceforth, I will commit my life to be your friend in Jesus Christ, the one who has touched us all and given our lives meaning.

We covenant together:

To apply our faith in all aspects of our lives;

To strive for a more perfect society in keeping with the Spirit of God;

To be faithful stewards of our time, influence, abilities, and possessions; to use them wisely and fully;

To assemble ourselves together regularly for worship, study, witness, and fellowship;

To pray for one another, and care for one another;

To encounter God daily through reading the Scriptures and prayer; and to be faithful to this fellowship of Christians.

Amen

4. ORDINANCES

Baptism and the Lord's Supper

Baptists adhere to the concept that Christ left two ordinances for Christians to follow. These ordinances are baptism and the Lord's Supper. Man did not originate these ordinances; they are of divine origin. Jesus participated in both ordinances during his ministry on earth. He told his disciples to follow his example. As Baptists follow the Scriptures for other spiritual foundations, so Baptists believe that both the biblical example and the method of these two ordinances should be followed.

Baptism and the Lord's Supper are ordinances rather than sacraments. Unlike sacraments, which some religious bodies believe to have saving qualities, ordinances are symbols that visualize and magnify the truths of the gospel.

Baptism

Most scholars agree that immersion was the mode of baptism acknowledged by Jesus and followed by the early church for several centuries. *Baptizo,* the Greek word for baptize, means to immerse or dip in water. The Scriptures bear out this definition. "And Jesus, when he was baptized went up straightway out of the water" (Matt. 3:16). The baptism of the eunuch by

Philip also confirms the idea of immersion. "And they went down both into the water, both Philip and the eunuch; and he baptized him. And when they were come up out of the water, the Spirit of the Lord caught away Philip" (Acts 8:38–39).

Only in later centuries did the practice of sprinkling develop as a matter of convenience.

Baptism is a symbolic act that pictures Christ's death, burial, and resurrection. A new Christian, as he is immersed, follows Christ's example in symbolizing his own death to sin, burial, and resurrection to a new life as a believer. "Buried with him in baptism, wherein also ye are risen with him through the faith of the operation of God, who hath raised him from the dead" (Col. 2:12). Through the symbolic act of baptism, an individual states that he has turned from sin to Christ. By the act of public baptism, the new Christian demonstrates to the world that he has been redeemed and is now a new person in Christ.

Baptism precedes the Lord's Supper. Christ was baptized by John the Baptist at the beginning of his earthly ministry. The Lord's Supper was instituted by Jesus prior to his crucifixion. Christians are to be reminded by the Lord's Supper of the broken body and the blood that was shed by Christ for the remission of their sins.

Lord's Supper

The Lord's Supper is not just a communion or fellowship between Christians but a time for each Christian to remember Christ. Jesus set the example for this memorial meal as he met with his followers prior to his crucifixion. He took a loaf of bread and prayed. He took the cup and prayed. The Scripture records: "And as they were eating, Jesus took bread, and blessed it, and brake it, and gave it to the disciples, and said, Take, eat; this is my body. And he took the cup, and gave thanks, and gave it to them, saying, Drink ye all of it; for this is my blood of the new testament [covenant], which is shed for many for the remission of sins" (Matt. 26:26–28).

Paul wrote to the church at Corinth: "For I have received of the Lord that which also I delivered unto you, That the Lord Jesus the same night in which he was betrayed took bread: and when he had given thanks, he brake it, and said, Take, eat: this is my body, which is broken for you: this do in remembrance of me. After the same manner also he took the cup, when he had supped, saying, This cup is the new testament [covenant] in my blood: this do ye, as oft as ye drink it, in remembrance of me. For as often as ye eat this bread, and drink this cup, ye do shew the Lord's death till he come" (1 Cor. 11:23–26).

Christ provided an ordinance of remembrance for Christians to follow. Believers are to remember Christ's love for man as they are reminded of his broken body and shed blood.

The Lord's Supper was first instituted by Christ with his closest followers. The meal was a solemn time of self-examination and celebration by persons who had followed Christ.

Some religious groups view the Lord's Supper as a

sacrament that has saving qualities. The Catholic Church views the bread and wine as magically changing into the actual body and blood of Christ when partaken.

Baptists have sought to remain close to the actual scriptural account. In doing so they follow Christ's command, "This do in remembrance of me."

5. DOCTRINE
Baptist Faith and Message

Throughout Baptist history, various Baptist groups have prepared and released statements of faith. These statements have served these bodies as a general consensus of doctrinal thought. At no time have these specific viewpoints been considered as formal creeds to be followed slavishly by all Baptists.

In 1925 the report of the Committee on Statement of Faith and Message was adopted by the Southern Baptist Convention. The committee report included an important introductory statement concerning the nature and function of confessions of faith in our religious and denominational life.

"(1) That they constitute a consensus of opinion of some Baptist body, large or small, for the general instruction and guidance of our own people and others concerning those articles of the Christian faith which are most surely held among us. They are not intended to add anything to the simple conditions of salvation revealed in the New Testament, viz., repentance towards God and faith in Jesus Christ as Saviour and Lord.

"(2) That we do not regard them as complete statements of our faith, having any quality of finality or infallibility. As in the past so in the future Baptists should hold themselves free to revise their statements of faith as may seem to them wise and expedient at any time.

"(3) That any group of Baptists, large or small have the inherent right to draw up for themselves and publish to the world a confession of their faith whenever they may think it advisable to do so.

"(4) That the sole authority for faith and practice among Baptists is the Scriptures of the Old and New Testaments. Confessions are only guides in interpretation, having no authority over the conscience.

"(5) That they are statements of religious convictions, drawn from the Scriptures, and are not to be used to hamper freedom of thought or investivation in other realms of life."

In 1963, the Southern Baptist Convention adopted a revised statement of Baptist Faith and Message prepared by a representative committee appointed in 1962.

The introductory statement of 1925 (above) was quoted as a part of the 1963 revision.

The following document seeks to provide a general consensus of Baptist doctrinal belief. It must be remembered, however, that the Baptist viewpoint concerning the priesthood of the believer, freedom in religious thought and practice, and soul competency before God allows each Baptist to formulate his own doctrinal interpretation. The copy of the statement below is a reproduction of a general tract published by the Sunday School Board and is used by permission.

THE BAPTIST FAITH AND MESSAGE

I. The Scriptures

The Holy Bible was written by men divinely inspired and is the record of God's revelation of Himself to man. It is a perfect treasure of divine instruction. It has God for its author, salvation for its end, and truth, without any mixture of error, for its matter. It reveals the principles by which God judges us; and therefore is, and will remain to the end of the world, the true center of Christian union, and the supreme standard by which all human conduct, creeds, and religious opinions should be tried. The criterion by which the Bible is to be interpreted is Jesus Christ.

Ex. 24:4; Deut. 4:1–2; 17:19; Josh. 8:34; Psalm 19:7–10; 119:11, 89, 105, 140; Isa. 34:16; 40:8; Jer. 15:16; 36; Matt. 5:17–18; 22:29; Luke 21:33; 24:44–46; John 5:39; 16:13–15; 17:17; Acts 2:16 ff.; 17:11; Rom. 15:4; 16:25–26; 2 Tim. 3:15–17; Heb. 1:1–2; 4:12; 1 Peter 1:25; 2 Peter 1:19–21

II. God

There is one and only one living and true God. He is an intelligent, spiritual, and personal Being, the Creator, Redeemer, Preserver, and Ruler of the universe. God is infinite in holiness and all other perfections. To Him we owe the highest love, reverence, and obedience. The eternal God reveals Himself to us as Father, Son, and Holy Spirit, with distinct personal attributes, but without division of nature, essence, or being.

A. God the Father

God as Father reigns with providential care over His universe, His creatures, and the flow of the stream of human history according to the purposes of His grace. He is all powerful, all loving, and all wise. God is Father in truth to those who become children of God through faith in Jesus Christ. He is fatherly in His attitude toward all men.

Gen. 1:1; 2:7; Ex. 3:14; 6:2–3; 15:11 ff.; 20:1 ff.; Lev. 22:2; Deut. 6:4; 32:6; 1 Chron. 29:10; Psalm 19:1–3; Isa. 43:3, 15; 64:8; Jer. 10:10; 17:13; Matt. 6:9 ff.; 7:11; 23:9; 28:19; Mark 1:9–11; John 4:24; 5:26; 14:6–13; 17:1–8; Acts 1:7; Rom. 8:14–15; 1 Cor. 8:6; Gal. 4:6; Eph. 4:6; Col. 1:15; 1 Tim. 1:17; Heb. 11:6; 12:9; 1 Peter 1:17; 1 John 5:7

B. God the Son

Christ is the eternal Son of God. In His incarnation as Jesus Christ he was conceived of the Holy Spirit and born of the virgin Mary. Jesus perfectly revealed and did the will of God, taking upon Himself the demands and necessities of human nature and identifying Himself completely with mankind yet without sin. He honored the divine law by His personal obedience, and in His death on the cross He made provision for the redemption of men from sin. He was raised from the dead with a glorified body and appeared to His disciples as the person who was with them before His crucifixion. He ascended into heaven and is now exalted at the right hand of God where He is the One Media-tor, partaking of the nature of God and of man, and in whose Person is effected the reconciliation between God and man. He will return in power and glory to judge the world and to consummate His redemptive mission. He now dwells in all believers as the living and ever present Lord.

Gen. 18:1 ff.; Psalm 2:7 ff.; 110:1 ff.; Isa. 7:14; 53; Matt. 1:18–23; 3:17; 8:29; 11:27; 14:33; 16:16, 27; 17:5; 27; 28:1–6, 19; Mark 1:1; 3:11; Luke 1:35; 4:41; 22:70; 24:46; John 1:1–18, 29; 10:30, 38; 11:25–27; 12:44–50; 14:7–11, 16:15–16, 28; 17:1–5, 21–22; 20: 1–20, 28; Acts 1:9; 2:22–24; 7:55–56; 9:4–5, 20; Rom. 1:3–4; 3:23–26; 5:6–21; 8:1–3, 34; 10:4; 1 Cor. 1:30; 2:2; 8:6; 15:1–8, 24–28; 2 Cor. 5:19–21; Gal. 4:4–5; Eph. 1:20; 3:11; 4:7–10; Phil. 2:5–11; Col. 1:13–22; 2:9; 1 Thess. 4:14–18; 1 Tim. 2:5–6; 3:16; Titus 2: 13–14; Heb. 1:1–3; 4:14–15; 7:14–28; 9:12–15, 24–28; 12:2; 13:8; 1 Peter 2:21–25; 3:22; 1 John 1:7–9; 3:2; 4:14–15; 5:9; 2 John 7–9; Rev. 1:13–16; 5:9–14; 12: 10–11; 13:8; 19:16

C. God the Holy Spirit

The Holy Spirit is the Spirit of God. He inspired holy men of old to write the Scriptures. Through illumination He enables men to understand truth. He exalts Christ. He convicts of sin, of righteousness and of judgment. He calls men to the Saviour, and effects regeneration. He cultivates Christian character, comforts believers, and bestows the spiritual gifts by which they serve God through His church. He seals the believer unto the day of final redemption. His presence in the Christian is the assurance of God to bring the believer into the fulness of the stature of Christ. He enlightens and empowers the believer and the church in worship, evangelism, and service.

Gen. 1:2; Judg. 14:6; Job 26:13; Psalm 51:11; 139: 7 ff.; Isa. 61:1–3; Joel 2:28–32; Matt. 1:18; 3:16; 4:1; 12:28–32; 28:19; Mark 1:10, 12; Luke 1:35; 4:1, 18–19; 11:13; 12:12; 24:49; John 4:24; 14:16–17, 26; 15:26; 16:7–14; Acts 1:8; 2:1–4, 38; 4:31; 5:3; 6:3; 7:55; 8:17, 39; 10:44; 13:2; 15:28; 16:6; 19:1–6; Rom. 8:9–11, 14–16, 26–27; 1 Cor. 2:10–14; 3:16; 12:3–11; Gal. 4:6; Eph. 1:13–14; 4:30; 5:18; 1 Thess. 5:19; 1 Tim. 3:16; 4:1; 2 Tim. 1:14; 3:16; Heb. 9:8, 14; 2 Peter 1–21; 1 John 4:13; 5:6–7; Rev. 1:10; 22:17

III. Man

Man was created by the special act of God, in His own image, and is the crowning work of His creation. In the beginning man was innocent of sin and was endowed by His Creator with freedom of choice. By his free choice man sinned against God and brought sin into the human race. Through the temptation of Satan man transgressed the command of God, and fell from his original innocence; whereby his posterity inherit a nature and an environment inclined toward sin, and as soon as they are capable of moral action become transgressors and are under condemnation. Only the grace of God can bring man into His holy fellowship and enable man to fulfill the creative purpose of God. The sacredness of human personality is evident in that God created man in His own image, and in that Christ died for man; therefore every man possesses dignity and is worthy of respect and Christian love.

Gen. 1:26–30; 2:5, 7, 18–22; 3; 9:6; Psalm 1; 8:3–6; 32:1–5; 51:5; Isa. 6:5; Jer. 17:5; Matt. 16:26; Acts 17: 26–31; Rom. 1:19–32; 3:10–18, 23; 5:6, 12, 19; 6:6; 7:14–25; 8:14–18, 29; 1 Cor. 1:21–31; 15:19, 21–22; Eph. 2:1–22; Col. 1:21–22; 3:9–11

IV. Salvation

Salvation involves the redemption of the whole man, and is offered freely to all who accept Jesus Christ as Lord and Saviour, who by His own blood obtained eternal redemption for the believer. In its broadest sense salvation includes regeneration, sanctification, and glorification.

A. Regeneration, or the new birth, is a work of God's grace whereby believers become new creatures in Christ Jesus. It is a change of heart wrought by the Holy Spirit through conviction of sin, to which the sinner responds in repentance toward God and faith in the Lord Jesus Christ.

Repentance and faith are inseparable experiences of grace. Repentance is a genuine turning from sin toward God. Faith is the acceptance of Jesus Christ and commitment of the entire personality to Him as Lord and Saviour. Justification is God's gracious and full acquittal upon principles of His righteousness of all sinners who repent and believe in Christ. Justification brings the believer into a relationship of peace and favor with God.

B. Sanctification is the experience, beginning in regeneration, by which the believer is set apart to God's purposes, and is enabled to progress toward moral and spiritual perfection through the presence and power of the Holy Spirit dwelling in him. Growth in grace should continue throughout the regenerate person's life.

C. Glorification is the culmination of salvation and is the final blessed and abiding state of the redeemed.

Gen. 3:15; Ex. 3:14–17; 6:2–8; Matt. 1:21; 4:17; 16:21–26; 27:22 to 28:6; Luke 1:68–69; 2:28–32; John 1:11–14, 29; 3:3–21, 36; 5:24; 10:9, 28–29; 15:1–16; 17:17; Acts 2:21; 4:12; 15:11; 16:30–31; 17:30–31; 20:32; Rom. 1:16–18; 2:4; 3:23–25; 4:3 ff.; 5:8–10; 6:1–23; 8:1–18; 29–39; 10:9–10, 13; 13:11–14; 1 Cor. 1:18, 30; 6:19–20; 15:10; 2 Cor. 5:17–20; Gal. 2:20; 3:13; 5:22–25; 6:15; Eph. 1:7; 2:8–22; 4:11–16; Phil. 2:12–13; Col. 1:9–22; 3:1 ff.; 1 Thess. 5:23–24; 2 Tim. 1:12; Titus 2:11–14; Heb. 2:1–3; 5:8–9; 9:24–28; 11:1 to 12:8, 14; James 2:14–26; 1 Peter 1:2–23; 1 John 1:6 to 2:11; Rev. 3:20; 21:1 to 22:5.

V. God's Purpose of Grace

Election is the gracious purpose of God, according to which He regenerates, sanctifies, and glorifies sinners. It is consistent with the free agency of man, and comprehends all the means of connection with the end. It is a glorious display of God's sovereign goodness, and is infinitely wise, holy, and unchangeable. It excludes boasting and promotes humility.

All true believers endure to the end. Those whom

God has accepted in Christ, and sanctified by His Spirit, will never fall away from the state of grace, but shall persevere to the end. Believers may fall into sin through neglect and temptation, whereby they grieve the Spirit, impair their graces and comforts, bring reproach on the cause of Christ, and temporal judgments on themselves, yet they shall be kept by the power of God through faith unto salvation.

Gen. 12:1–3; Ex. 19:5–8; 1 Sam. 8:4–7, 19–22; Isa. 5:1–7; Jer. 31:31 ff.; Matt. 16:18–19; 21:28–45; 24:22, 31; 25:34; Luke 1:68–79; 2:29–32; 19:41–44; 24:44–48; John 1:12–14; 3:16; 5:24; 6:44–45, 65; 10:27–29; 15:16; 17:6, 12, 17–18; Acts 20:32; Rom. 5:9–10; 8:28–39; 10:12–15; 11:5–7, 26–36; 1 Cor. 1:1–2; 15:24–28; Eph. 1:4–23; 2:1–10; 3:1–11; Col. 1:12–14; 2 Thess. 2:13–14; 2 Tim. 1:12; 2:10, 19; Heb. 11:39 to 12:2; 1 Peter 1:2–5, 13; 2:4–10; 1 John 1:7–9; 2:19; 3:2

VI. The Church

A New Testament church of the Lord Jesus Christ is a local body of baptized believers who are associated by covenant in the faith and fellowship of the gospel, observing the two ordinances of Christ, committed to His teachings, exercising the gifts, rights, and privileges invested in them by His Word, and seeking to extend the gospel to the ends of the earth.

This church is an autonomous body, operating through democratic processes under the Lordship of Jesus Christ. In such a congregation members are equally responsible. Its Scriptural officers are pastors and deacons.

The New Testament speaks also of the church as the body of Christ which includes all of the redeemed of all the ages.

Matt. 16:15–19; 18:15–20; Acts 2:41–42, 47; 5: 11–14; 6:3–6; 13:1–3; 14:23, 27; 15:1–30; 16:5; 20:28; Rom. 1:7; 1 Cor. 1:2; 3:16; 5:4–5; 7:17; 9:13–14; 12; Eph. 1:22–23; 2:19–22; 3:8–11, 21; 5:22–32; Phil. 1:1; Col. 1:18; 1 Tim. 3:1–15; 4:14; 1 Peter 5:1–4; Rev. 2–3; 21:2–3

VII. Baptism and the Lord's Supper

Christian baptism is the immersion of a believer in water in the name of the Father, the Son, and the Holy Spirit. It is an act of obedience symbolizing the believer's faith in a crucified, buried, and risen Saviour, the believer's death to sin, the burial of the old life, and the resurrection to walk in newness of life in Christ Jesus. It is a testimony to his faith in the final resurrection of the dead. Being a church ordinance, it is prerequisite to the privileges of church membership and to the Lord's Supper.

The Lord's Supper is a symbolic act of obedience whereby members of the church, through partaking of the bread and the fruit of the vine, memorialize the death of the Redeemer and anticipate His second coming.

Matt. 3:13–17; 26:26–30; 28:19–20; Mark 1:9–11; 14:22–26; Luke 3:21–22; 22:19–20; John 3:23; Acts 2:41–42; 8:35–39; 16:30–33; Acts 20:7; Rom. 6:3–5; 1 Cor. 10:16, 21; 11:23–29; Col. 2:12

VIII. The Lord's Day

The first day of the week is the Lord's Day. It is a Christian institution for regular observance. It commemorates the resurrection of Christ from the dead and should be employed in exercises of worship and spiritual devotion, both public and private, and by refraining from worldly amusements, and resting from secular employment, work of necessity and mercy only being excepted.

Ex. 20:8–11; Matt. 12:1–12; 28:1 ff.; Mark 2:27–28; 16:1–7; Luke 24:1–3, 33–36; John 4:21–24; 20:1, 19–28; Acts 20:7; 1 Cor. 16:1–2; Col. 2:16; 3:16; Rev. 1:10

IX. The Kingdom

The Kingdom of God includes both His general sovereignty over the universe and His particular kingship over men who willfully acknowledge Him as King. Particularly the Kingdom is the realm of salvation into which men enter by trustful, childlike commitment to Jesus Christ. Christians ought to pray and to labor that the Kingdom may come and God's will be done on earth. The full consummation of the Kingdom awaits the return of Jesus Christ and the end of this age.

Gen. 1:1; Isa. 9:6–7; Jer. 23:5–6; Matt. 3:2; 4:8–10, 23; 12:25–28; 13:1–52; 25:31–46; 26:29; Mark 1: 14–15; 9:1; Luke 4:43; 8:1; 9:2; 12:31–32; 17:20–21; 23:42; John 3:3; 18:36; Acts 1:6–7; 17:22–31; Rom. 5:17; 8:19; 1 Cor. 15:24–28; Col. 1:13; Heb. 11:10, 16;

12:28; 1 Peter 2:4–10; 4:13; Rev. 1:6, 9; 5:10; 11:15; 21–22

X. Last Things

God, in His own time and in His own way, will bring the world to its appropriate end. According to His promise, Jesus Christ will return personally and visibly in glory to the earth; the dead will be raised; and Christ will judge all men in righteousness. The unrighteous will be consigned to Hell, the place of everlasting punishment. The righteous in their resurrection and glorified bodies will receive their reward and will dwell forever in Heaven with the Lord.

Isa. 2:4; 11:9; Matt. 16:27; 18:8–9; 19:28; 24:27, 30, 36, 44; 25:31–46; 26:64; Mark 8:38; 9:43–48; Luke 12:40, 48; 16:19–26; 17:22–37; 21:27–28; John 14: 1–3; Acts 1:11; 17:31; Rom. 14:10; 1 Cor. 4:5; 15: 24–28, 35–58; 2 Cor. 5:10; Phil. 3:20–21; Col. 1:5; 3:4; 1 Thess. 4:14–18; 5:1 ff.; 2 Thess. 1:7 ff.; 2; 1 Tim. 6:14; 2 Tim. 4:1, 8; Titus 2:13; Heb. 9:27–28; James 5:8; 2 Peter 3:7 ff.; 1 John 2:28; 3:2; Jude 14; Rev. 1:18; 3:11; 20:1 to 22:13

XI. Evangelism and Missions

It is the duty and privilege of every follower of Christ and of every church of the Lord Jesus Christ to endeavor to make disciples of all nations. The new birth of man's spirit by God's Holy Spirit means the birth of love for others. Missionary effort on the part of all rests thus upon a spiritual necessity of the regenerate life, and is expressly and repeatedly commanded in the teachings of Christ. It is the duty of every child of God to seek constantly to win the lost to Christ by personal effort and by all other methods in harmony with the gospel of Christ.

Gen. 12:1–3; Ex. 19:5–6; Isa. 6:1–8; Matt. 9:37–38; 10:5–15; 13:18–30, 37–43; 16:19; 22:9–10; 24:14; 28: 18–20; Luke 10:1–18; 24:46–53; John 14:11–12; 15: 7–8, 16; 17:15; 20:21; Acts 1:8; 2; 8:26–40; 10:42–48; 13:2–3; Rom. 10:13–15; Eph. 3:1–11; 1 Thess. 1:8; 2 Tim. 4:5; Heb. 2:1–3; 11:39 to 12:2; 1 Peter 2:4–10; Rev. 22:17

XII. Education

The cause of education in the Kingdom of Christ is co-ordinate with the causes of missions and general benevolence, and should receive along with these the liberal support of the churches. An adequate system of Christian schools is necessary to a complete spiritual program for Christ's people.

In Christian education there should be a proper balance between academic freedom and academic responsibility. Freedom in any orderly relationship of human life is always limited and never absolute. The freedom of a teacher in a Christian school, college, or seminary is limited by the pre-eminence of Jesus Christ, by the authoritative nature of the Scriptures, and by the distinct purpose for which the school exists.

Deut. 4:1, 5, 9, 14; 6:1–10; 31:12–13; Neh. 8:1–8; Job 28:28; Psalm 19:7 ff.; 119:11; Prov. 3:13 ff.; 4: 1–10; 8:1–7, 11; 15:14; Eccl. 7:19; Matt. 5:2; 7:24 ff.; 28:19–20; Luke 2:40; 1 Cor. 1:18–31; Eph. 4:11–16;

Phil. 4:8; Col. 2:3, 8–9; 1 Tim. 1:3–7; 2 Tim. 2:15;
3:14–17; Heb. 5:12 to 6:3; James 1:5; 3:17

XIII. Stewardship

God is the source of all blessings, temporal and
spiritual; all that we have and are we owe to Him.
Christians have a spiritual debtorship to the whole
world, a holy trusteeship in the gospel, and a binding
stewardship in their possessions. They are therefore
under obligation to serve him with their time, talents,
and material possessions; and should recognize all
these as entrusted to them to use for the glory of God
and for helping others. According to the Scriptures,
Christians should contribute of their means cheerfully, regularly, systematically, proportionately, and
liberally for the advancement of the Redeemer's cause
on earth.

Gen. 14:20; Lev. 27:30–32; Deut. 8:18; Mal. 3:8–12;
Matt. 6:1–4, 19–21; 19:21; 23:23; 25:14–29; Luke 12:
16–21, 42; 16:1–13; Acts 2:44–47; 5:1–11; 17:24–25;
20:35; Rom. 6:6–22; 12:1–2; 1 Cor. 4:1–2; 6:19–20; 12;
16:1–4; 2 Cor. 8–9; 12:15; Phil. 4:10–19; 1 Peter 1:
18–19

XIV. Cooperation

Christ's people should, as occasion requires, organize such associations and conventions as may best secure cooperation for the great objects of the Kingdom
of God. Such organizations have no authority over one
another or over the churches. They are voluntary and
advisory bodies designed to elicit, combine, and direct

the energies of our people in the most effective manner. Members of New Testament churches should cooperate with one another in carrying forward the missionary, educational, and benevolent ministries for the extension of Christ's Kingdom. Christian unity in the New Testament sense is spiritual harmony and voluntary cooperation for common ends by various groups of Christ's people. Cooperation is desirable between the various Christian denominations, when the end to be attained is itself justified, and when such cooperation involves no violation of conscience or compromise of loyalty to Christ and His Word as revealed in the New Testament.

Ex. 17:12; 18:17 ff.; Judg. 7:21; Ezra 1:3–4; 2:68–69; 5:14–15; Neh. 4; 8:1–5; Matt. 10:5–15; 20:1–16; 22:1–10; 28:19–20; Mark 2:3; Luke 10:1 ff.; Acts 1:13–14; 2:1 ff.; 4:31–37; 13:2–3; 15:1–35; 1 Cor. 1:10–17; 3:5–15; 12; 2 Cor. 8–9; Gal. 1:6–10; Eph. 4:1–16; Phil. 1:15–18

XV. The Christian and the Social Order

Every Christian is under obligation to seek to make the will of Christ supreme in his own life and in human society. Means and methods used for the improvement of society and the establishment of righteousness among men can be truly and permanently helpful only when they are rooted in the regeneration of the individual by the saving grace of God in Christ Jesus. The Christian should oppose in the spirit of Christ every form of greed, selfishness, and vice. He should work to provide for the orphaned, the needy, the aged, the helpless, and the sick. Every Christian should seek to bring industry, government, and society as a whole under the sway of of the principles of righteousness, truth, and brotherly love. In order to promote these ends Christians should be ready to work with all men of good will in any good cause, always being careful to act in the spirit of love without compromising their loyalty to Christ and His truth.

Ex. 20:3–17; Lev. 6:2–5; Deut. 10:12; 27:17; Psalm 101:5; Mic. 6:8; Zech. 8:16; Matt. 5:13–16, 43–48; 22:36–40; 25:35; Mark 1:29–34; 2:3 ff.; 10:21; Luke 4:18–21; 10:27–37; 20:25; John 15:12; 17:15; Rom. 12–14; 1 Cor. 5:9–10; 6:1–7; 7:20–24; 10:23 to 11:1; Gal. 3:26–28; Eph. 6:5–9; Col. 3:12–17; 1 Thess. 3:12; Philemon; James 1:27; 2:8

XVI. Peace and War

It is the duty of Christians to seek peace with all men on principles of righteousness. In accordance with the spirit and teachings of Christ they should do all in their power to put an end to war.

The true remedy for the war spirit is the gospel of our Lord. The supreme need of the world is the acceptance of His teachings in all the affairs of men and nations, and the practical application of His law of love.

Isa. 2:4; Matt. 5:9, 38–48; 6:33; 26:52; Luke 22:36, 38; Rom. 12:18–19; 13:1–7; 14:19; Heb. 12:14; James 4:1–2

XVII. Religious Liberty

God alone is Lord of the conscience, and He has left it free from the doctrines and commandments of men which are contrary to His Word or not contained in it. Church and state should be separate. The state owes to every church protection and full freedom in the pursuit of its spiritual ends. In providing for such freedom no ecclesiastical group or denomination should be favored by the state more than others. Civil government being ordained of God, it is the duty of Christians to render loyal obedience thereto in all things not contrary to the revealed will of God. The church should not resort to the civil power to carry on its work. The gospel of Christ contemplates spiritual means alone for the pursuit of its ends. The state has no right to impose penalties for religious opinions of any kind. The state has no right to impose taxes for the support of any form of religion. A free church in a free state is the Christian ideal, and this implies the right of free and unhindered access to God on the part of all men, and the right to form and propagate opinions in the sphere of religion without interference by the civil power.

Gen. 1:27; 2:7; Matt. 6:6–7, 24; 16:26; 22:21; John 8:36; Acts 4:19–20; Rom. 6:1–2; 13:1–7; Gal. 5:1, 13; Phil. 3:20; 1 Tim. 2:1–2; James 4:12; 1 Peter 2:12–17; 3:11–17; 4:12–19

6. CHURCH ORGANIZATION
How to Organize for Growth

Organization provides the structure needed by a church for mobilizing its resources to move toward the attainment of its basic spiritual purpose. Organization structure is a means to an end rather than an end in itself. Organization provides handles by which a church involves its members meaningfully in its life and work. Organization enables a church to group its work into manageable parts.

Some persons express a distrust of organization. Others voice the opinion that churches have too much organization structure. These individuals, unfortunately, do not understand organization.

Organization is similar to digestion, for it works quietly and effectively in performing its unique purpose. An individual, for example, does not think about his digestive processes until digestion ceases to work properly. The problem, actually, is one of indigestion rather than digestion.

So it is with church organization structure. When organization becomes oppressively apparent, the problem is usually one of disorganization rather than organization.

Below are some principles to help a church organize for growth.

- Keep organization structure as simple as possible.
- Group similar jobs or work together.
- Keep organization structure as flexible as possible.
- Organization structure should help achieve goals, objectives, and basic mission or purpose.
- Organization should provide for optimum communication.
- Organization structure should not require more leaders than are available.
- Provide each organization and organizational leader a written statement of responsibilities.
- Organization structure should allow decisions to be made at appropriate level.
- Develop and provide a written organization chart.
- Develop and provide a written job description for each person in the organization structure.
- Organization should be easily expandable.
- Organization structure should provide for adequate coordination.

Steps in Organization Structure

How does a new church go about organizing itself to get its work accomplished? How does an established church reorganize itself?

The following steps are essential to a sound organization structure.

1. *Develop Statement of Church Purpose*

The initial step in establishing the organization structure of a church is to prepare a brief statement

of purpose. A statement of church purpose provides
a biblical foundation that answers why a church exists.
A purpose statement is like a concrete and steel foundation resting on solid rock. By knowing its basic
spiritual purpose, a church takes the first step in determining how to organize its work.

Each church should develop its own purpose rather
than copying the purpose statement of another
church.

2. *Develop Church Objectives*

Objectives grow out of a church's purpose. Objectives tell the ultimate outcome a church is trying to
achieve through all its activities. Long-range objectives are like the North Star that provides a firm direction for the traveler. A statement of objectives provides a church with spiritual direction so that all
decisions are made in light of the question, Will this
action lead us toward our ultimate objective? Some
churches have developed a single objective while others have developed multiple statements.

3. *Develop Statement of Church Tasks*

Church tasks are those ongoing areas of work that
a New Testament church must fulfil if it is to move
toward achieving its objectives. The early churches
had little organization structure, but they did perform
certain ongoing work that was essential to being a
church. They worshiped, proclaimed the gospel, min-
istered to needs, sang God's praises, trained for service, and participated in mission endeavors.

Every church today has responsibility, for example, for teaching how God revealed himself through Jesus Christ. This teaching of biblical revelation is an ongoing responsibility of primary importance that moves a church toward the attainment of its spiritual objectives. Likewise, churches must train and nurture members and leaders, teach missions, proclaim the gospel to believers and unbelievers, and sing praises to God.

A church, in the light of its purpose and objectives, must determine its ongoing spiritual tasks.

4. *Group Tasks into Organizational Units*

Baptist churches have traditionally organized their basic ongoing work (tasks) into (1) church program organizations, (2) church program services, and (3) church administrative services.

Church Program Organizations

Five basic church program organizations are found in Baptist churches. These program organizations are responsible to the church, and leaders are recommended by the church nominating committee and elected by the church.

(1) *Sunday School.*—The basic purpose of Sunday School is outreach and Bible teaching. The Sunday School has proven itself an effective organization for reaching people for Christ and for teaching how God revealed himself in Jesus Christ.

The administrative leader is the Sunday School director. Tasks of Sunday School are:

Teach the biblical revelation

Reach persons for Christ and church membership

Perform the functions of worship, witness, education, and ministry

Provide and interpret information regarding the work of the church and denomination

(2) *Training Union.*—The basic purpose of Training Union is to train church members and church leaders. The church training program has made a major contribution in providing training on Sunday night in Baptist churches. Church Training can also take place anytime during the week.

The administrative leader is the church training director. Tasks of Training Union are:

Orient new church members

Train church members to perform the functions of the church

Train church leaders

Teach Christian theology, Christian ethics, Christian history, and church polity and organization

Provide and interpret information regarding the work of the church and denomination

(3) *Church Music.*—The basic responsibility of Church Music is to provide music for the church.

The administrative leader is the Church Music director. Tasks of Church Music are:

Teach music

Train persons to sing, play, and lead music

Provide music for the church and the community

Provide and interpret information regarding the work of the church and denomination

(4) *Woman's Missionary Union.*—The basic responsi-

bility of the Woman's Missionary Union is to study missions and to participate in mission action.

The administrative leader is the Woman's Missionary Union director. Tasks of Woman's Missionary Union are:

Teach missions

Engage in mission action

Support world missions through praying and giving

Provide and interpret information regarding the work of the church and denomination

(5) *Brotherhood.*—The basic responsibility of the Brotherhood is to study missions and to participate in mission action.

The administrative leader is the Brotherhood director. Tasks of the Brotherhood Program are:

Teach missions

Engage in mission action

Support world missions through praying and giving

Provide and interpret information regarding the work of the church and denomination

Church Program Services

Church Library and Church Recreation are classified as church program services. These program services provide support to the leaders and members of the church program organization as well as church officers and committees.

(1) *Church library service.*—The primary responsibility of the church library service is to serve as a resource center for the church.

The church library staff is recommended by the

nominating committee and elected by the church. The library staff is composed of the number required to meet the needs of the church.

The director of library services is the administrative leader of the church library service. Tasks of church library service are:

Provide printed and audiovisual resources

Promote the use of printed and audiovisual resources

Consult with church leaders and members in the use of printed and audiovisual resources

(2) *Church recreation service.*—The primary responsibility of the church recreation service is to assist the church to meet the recreation needs of the members and groups.

The church recreation staff is recommended by the nominating committee and elected by the church. The recreation staff is composed of the number required to meet the needs of the church.

The recreation director is the administrative leader of the church recreation service. Tasks of the church recreation service are:

Provide recreation

Provide consultation, leadership assistance, and resources in recreation

(3) *Church administrative services.*—Administrative service work in a church is usually conducted by church officers and committees. Administrative services help the church achieve its total administrative work by providing specialized services that the entire

congregation needs in order to do its work. Administrative services assist all program organizations and program services in such matters as finances, properties, personnel, and food services.

Administrative services personnel (church officers and committee members) are recommended by the nominating committee and elected by the church. Tasks of administrative services are:

Assist the church to plan, coordinate, and evaluate its life and work

Assist the church to secure, allocate, and account for its resources

Assist the church in governing its life and work under the lordship of Christ

Church Grouping and Grading Patterns

A church must organize its work to achieve its own goals and objectives. Organization should be a means to an end rather than an end in itself.

Through experience, Baptist churches have discovered that certain patterns of organization work more effectively than others. Basic curriculum materials are developed by denominational agencies that follow common organizational approaches. Though churches will decide on their own organizational structure, there is a wide acceptance of the following grouping-grading plan being followed by Southern Baptist agencies that produce curriculum materials.

The grouping-grading plan provides for four basic divisions:

Preschool Division—Birth through five years

Children's Division—Six (Grade 1) through eleven
  years (Grade 6)

Youth Division—Twelve (Grade 7) through seven-
  teen years (Grade 12)

Adult Division—Eighteen (High School Gradua-
  tion) and up

- Young Adult—Eighteen (High School Gradua-
  tion) through twenty-nine Years

- Adult—Thirty through fifty-nine (or retirement)

- Senior Adult—Sixty and up

Using these four basic divisions, churches of all sizes
can determine their appropriate plan for grading. The
small church should have four separate classes based
on the four major divisions (Preschool, Children,
Youth, and Adult). The large church could provide for
multiple departments or classes. This divisional plan
for grouping-grading is highly flexible.

Churches generally use the local public school en-
trance date as the suggested date for use in classifying
preschoolers, children, and youth. The date usually
followed for classifying adults is January 1. October
1 is the most popularly used date for promotion.

7. CHURCH CONSTITUTION AND BYLAWS
Legal Requirements

A constitution and bylaws provides written guidelines to assist a church in moving toward the attainment of its divine purpose.

A church constitution and bylaws usually contains a basic statement of purpose or objective, the legal name of the church, a statement of doctrinal belief, and a statement of basic relationships. The bylaws usually state how a church is organized to conduct its work, qualifications for membership, congregational procedures for conducting church business, and duties of the church program organization leaders. Such a document is not imperative, but churches have found that a constitution and bylaws can be helpful in conducting its work effectively.

Another legal relationship that churches need to understand is the process of incorporation.

When a church is incorporated, it becomes a legal entity. Church members and church trustees cannot be held responsible for personal liability when they act in their corporate capacity after receiving formal instructions from the church.

In the eyes of the law, an unincorporated church has no legal status. It does not have the power to sue or be sued. Trustees of an unincorporated church are held personally responsible for any legal notes they may sign for the church. Even if a church trustee moves his membership to another church, he is still legally liable if his name appears on legal documents from the unincorporated church. Signing a legal document for an incorporated church, on the other hand, does not make one personally liable.

It is relatively easy and inexpensive for a church to be incorporated. An attorney should be consulted to handle the legal work.

Sample Constitution and Bylaws

The following material was published by the Sunday School Board in 1970 as a booklet under the title *How to Develop a Church Constitution and Bylaws* and is used here by permission.

CONSTITUTION

Preamble

We declare and establish this constitution to preserve and secure the principles of our faith, and to govern the body in an orderly manner. This constitution will preserve the liberties of each individual church member and the freedom of action of this body in its relation to other churches.

I. Name

This body shall be known as the _____ _____ Baptist Church of _____, located at _____.

II. Objectives

To be a dynamic spiritual organism empowered by the Holy Spirit to share Christ with as many people as possible in our church, community, and throughout the world.

To be a worshiping fellowship, experiencing an awareness of God, recognizing his person, and responding in obedience to his leadership.

To experience an increasingly meaningful fellowship.with God and fellow believers.

To help people experience a growing knowledge of God and man.

To be a church that ministers unselfishly to persons in the community and world in Jesus' name.

To be a church whose purpose is to be Christlike in our daily living by emphasizing total commitment of life, personality, and possessions to the lordship of Christ.

III. Statement of Faith

The Holy Bible is the inspired word of God and is the basis for any statement of faith. The church subscribes to the doctrinal statement of "The Baptist Faith and Message" as adopted by the Southern Baptist Convention in 1963. We band ourselves together as a body of baptized believers in Jesus Christ personally committed to sharing the good news of salvation to lost mankind. The ordinances of the church are baptism and the Lord's Supper.

IV. Relationships

The government of this church is vested in the body of believers who compose it. It is subject to the control of no other ecclesiastical body, but it recognizes and sustains the obligations of mutual counsel and cooperation which are common among Baptist churches. Insofar as is practical, this church will cooperate with and support the association and state convention affiliated with the Southern Baptist Convention.

V. Church Covenant

Having been led, as we believe, by the Spirit of God, to receive the Lord Jesus Christ as our Saviour and Lord and, on the profession of our faith, having been baptized in the name of the Father, and of the Son, and of the Holy Spirit, we do now, in the presence of God, and this assembly, most solemnly and joyfully enter into covenant with one another as one body in Christ.

We engage, therefore, by the aid of the Holy Spirit to walk together in Christian love; to strive for the advancement of this church, in knowledge, holiness, and comfort; to promote its prosperity and spirituality; to sustain its worship, ordinances, discipline, and doctrines; to contribute cheerfully and regularly to the support of the ministry, the expenses of the church, the relief of the poor, and the spread of the gospel through all nations.

We also engage to maintain family and secret devotions; to religiously educate our children; to seek the salvation of our kindred and acquaintances; to walk circumspectly in the world; to be just in our dealings, faithful in our engagements, and exemplary in our deportment; to avoid all tattling, backbiting, and excessive anger; to abstain from the sale of and use of intoxicating drinks as a beverage; to use our influence to combat the abuse of drugs and the spread of pornography; and to be zealous in our efforts to advance the kingdom of our Saviour.

We further engage to watch over one another in brotherly love; to remember one another in prayer; to aid one another in sickness and distress; to cultivate Christian sympathy in feeling and Christian courtesy in speech; to be slow to take offense, but always ready for reconciliation and mindful of the rules of our Saviour to secure it without delay.

We moreover engage that when we remove from this place we will, as soon as possible, unite with some other church where we can carry out the spirit of this covenant and the principles of God's Word.

BYLAWS

I. Membership

Section 1. General

This is a sovereign and democratic Baptist church under the lordship of Jesus Christ. The membership retains unto itself the exclusive right of self-government in all phases of the spiritual and temporal life of this church.

The membership reserves the exclusive right to de-

termine who shall be members of this church and the
conditions of such membership.

Section 2. Candidacy

Any person may offer himself as a candidate for
membership in this church. All such candidates shall
be presented to the church at any regular church service for membership in any of the following ways:

(1) By profession of faith and for baptism according
to the policies of this church

(2) By promise of a letter of recommendation from
another Baptist church

(3) By restoration upon a statement of prior conversion experience and baptism in a Baptist church
when no letter is obtainable

Should there be any dissent as to any candidate,
such dissent shall be referred to the pastor and the
deacons for investigation and the making of a recommendation to the church within thirty (30) days. A
three-fourths vote of those church members present
and voting shall be required to elect such candidates
to membership.

Section 3. New Member Orientation

New church members will be expected to participate in the church's new member orientation plan.

Section 4. Voting Rights of Members

Every member of the church is entitled to vote at
all elections and on all questions submitted to the
church in conference, provided the member is present
or provision has been made for absentee balloting.

Section 5. Termination of Membership

Membership shall be terminated in the following ways: (1) death, (2) dismission to another Baptist church, (3) exclusion by action of this church.

Section 6. Discipline

(1) It shall be the basic purpose of the _____ Baptist Church to emphasize to its members that every reasonable measure will be taken to assist any troubled member. The pastor, other members of the church staff, and deacons are available for counsel and guidance. Redemption rather than punishment should be the guideline which governs the attitude of one member toward another.

(2) Should some serious condition exist which would cause a member to become a liability to the general welfare of the church, every reasonable measure will be taken by the pastor and by the deacons to resolve the problem. All such proceedings shall be pervaded by a spirit of Christian kindness and forbearance. But, finding that the welfare of the church will best be served by the exclusion of the member, the church may take this action by a two-thirds vote of the members present at a meeting called for this purpose; and the church may proceed to declare the offender to be no longer in the membership of the church.

(3) Any person whose membership has been terminated for any condition which has made it necessary for the church to exclude him may upon his request be restored to membership by a vote of the church upon evidence of his repentance and reformation.

II. Church Officers

All church officers must be members of the church. The officers of this church shall be as follows:

Section 1. Pastor

The pastor is responsible for leading the church to function as a New Testament church. The pastor will lead the congregation, the organizations, and the church staff to perform their tasks.

The pastor is leader of pastoral ministries in a church. As such he works with the deacons and church staff to: (1) lead the church in the achievement of its mission, (2) proclaim the gospel to believers and unbelievers, and (3) care for the church's members and other persons in the community.

A pastor shall be chosen and called by the church whenever a vacancy occurs. His election shall take place at a meeting called for that purpose, of which at least one week's public notice has been given.

A pastor selection committee shall be appointed by the church to seek out a pastor, and its recommendations will constitute a nomination. Any member has the privilege of making other nominations according to the policy established by the church. The committee shall bring to the consideration of the church only one name at a time. Election shall be by ballot, an affirmative vote of three fourths of those present being necessary for a choice. The pastor, thus elected, shall serve until the relationship is terminated by his request or the church's request. He shall preside at meetings of the church. The pastor shall give at least two weeks notice at the time of resignation before terminating his responsibilities as pastor.

Section 2. Church Staff

This church shall call or employ such staff members as the church shall need. A job description shall be written when the need for staff members is determined. Vocational staff members other than the pastor shall be recommended to the church by the personnel committee and employed by church action. At least two weeks notice at this time of resignation should be given.

The secretaries and custodians shall likewise be recommended to the church by the personnel committee and employed by church action.

Section 3. Deacons

(1) There shall be one deacon for every fifteen church families. Deacons shall be elected at regular business meetings of the church by secret ballot.

The deacons shall serve on a rotation basis. Each year the term of office of one third of the number of deacons shall expire, and election shall be held to fill the vacancies. In case of death or removal or incapacity to serve, the church may elect a deacon to fill the unexpired term. After serving a term of three years, a deacon shall be eligible for reelection only after the lapse of at least one year. There is no obligation to constitute as an active deacon a person who comes to the church from another church where he has served as deacon.

(2) In accordance with the meaning of the work and the practice of the New Testament, deacons are to be servants of the church. The task of the deacon is to serve with the pastor and staff in performing pastoral ministries tasks: proclaim the gospel to believers and unbelievers; care for church members and other persons in the community; lead the church to achieve its mission.

Section 4. Moderator

The moderator shall be elected annually. In the absence of the moderator, the chairman of deacons shall preside; or in the absence of both, the clerk shall call the church to order and an acting moderator shall be elected.

Section 5. Clerk

The church-elected clerk of the church shall keep in a suitable book a record of all the actions of the church, except as otherwise herein provided. He is responsible for keeping a register of the names of members, with dates of admission, dismission, or death, together with a record of baptisms. He shall issue letters of dismission voted by the church, preserve on file all communications and written official reports, and give legal notice of all meetings where such notice is necessary, as indicated in these bylaws. The church may delegate some of the clerical responsibilities to a church secretary. All church records are church property and should be filed in the church office when an office is maintained.

Section 6. Treasurer

The church shall elect annually a church treasurer. It shall be the duty of the treasurer to receive, preserve, and pay out, upon receipt of vouchers approved and signed by authorized personnel, all money, or things of value paid or given to the church, keeping at all times an itemized account of all receipts and disbursements. It shall be the duty of the treasurer to render to the church at each regular business meeting an itemized report of the receipts and disbursements for the preceding month. The treasurer's report shall be audited annually by an auditing committee or public accountant. The treasurer shall be bonded.

Upon rendering the annual account at the end of each fiscal year, and its acceptance and approval by the church, the records shall be delivered by the treasurer to the church clerk, who shall keep and preserve the account as a part of the permanent records of the church.

Section 7. Trustees

Three trustees elected by the church will hold in trust the church property. They shall have no power to buy, sell, mortgage, lease, or transfer any property without a specific vote of the church authorizing each action. It shall be the function of the trustees to affix their signatures to legal documents involving the sale, mortgage, purchase, or rental of property or other legal documents where the signatures of trustees are required. Trustees shall serve on a rotating basis, with one new trustee being elected every three years.

III. Committees and Coordinating Groups

Section 1.   General

All church committee members shall be recommended by the nominating committee and elected by the church unless otherwise indicated in the description below. The committee members shall serve on a three-year rotation system with one third to be elected each year.

Section 2.   Church Council

(1) The primary functions of the council shall be to recommend to the congregation suggested objectives and church goals; to review and coordinate program plans recommended by church officers, organizations, and committees; to recommend to the congregation the use of leadership, calendar time, and other resources according to program priorities; and to evaluate program achievements in terms of church goals and objectives.

(2) The council, unless otherwise determined by vote of the church, shall have as regular members the pastor, minister of education, minister of music, Sunday School director, Training Union director, Woman's Missionary Union director, Brotherhood director, and chairman of deacons. Committee chairmen and church-elected officers shall serve as ex officio members.

(3) All matters agreed upon by the council, calling for action not already authorized, shall be referred to the church for approval or disapproval.

Section 3.   Nominating Committee

The nominating committee coordinates the staffing of all church leadership positions that are filled by volunteers. The nominating committee recommends persons for all volunteer positions to be elected by the church.

Section 4.   Personnel Committee

The personnel committee assists the church in matters related to employed personnel administration. Its work includes such areas as determining staff needs, employment, salaries, benefits, and personnel services.

Section 5.   Properties and Space Committee

The properties committee assists the church in matters related to properties administration. Its work includes such areas as maintaining all church properties for ready use, recommending policies regarding use of properties, recommending employment of maintenance personnel, and assigning responsibility to appropriate personnel for supervision.

Section 6.   Stewardship Committee

The stewardship committee develops and recommends an overall stewardship information plan and administers the gifts of church members, using sound principles of financial management.

Section 7.   Missions Committee

The missions committee seeks to discover possibilities for local missions projects, shares findings with church program organizations, and serves the church in establishing and conducting such missions projects as may be assigned to it.

Section 8.   Public Relations Committee

The public relations committee is to discover the public relations needs and choose the means of communication to persons inside and outside the church. The committee is responsible for discovering what needs to be communicated and for communicating with the proper audience.

Section 9.   Kitchen Committee

The kitchen committee is responsible for formulating and recommending to the church policies for the kitchen and for communicating these policies to church members.

Section 10.   Kindergarten Committee

The church kindergarten committee is to study the needs for, and possibilities of, a church kindergarten program, to help in the organization of this program where it is considered wise, and to serve as a liaison between the church and the kindergarten.

Section 11.   Church Ushers

Every regular church usher shall be selected by the nominating committee and elected by the church. The ushers shall be led by an usher chairman, also selected by the nominating committee and elected by the church. The ushers are to greet people as they enter and leave the church, seat people at the proper time, provide bulletins and/or other materials at the time of seating. The ushers will be attentive to the needs of the congregation and the pastor.

Section 12. History Committee

The history committee is to preserve and use the historical records of the church. The committee is especially concerned with gathering and preserving available church records, recording full and accurate records, and using the records to help members understand and appreciate their heritage and mission.

Section 13. Flower Committee

The flower committee is responsible for securing, arranging, and disposing of floral arrangements for church services and for providing flowers for sick and bereaved members.

IV. Program Services

Section 1. General

The staff of program services shall be recommended by the church nominating committee for election by the church.

Section 2. Church Recreation Service

The recreation staff will serve the church in seeking to meet the recreational needs of members and groups. They will provide recreation activities and

provide consultation, leadership assistance, and resources.

Section 3. Church Library Service

The church library will serve as the resource center
for the church. The church library staff will seek to
provide and promote the use of printed and audiovisual resources. The staff will also provide consultation to church leaders and members in the use of
printed and audiovisual resources.

V. Program Organizations

Section 1. General

All organizations of the church shall be under
church control, all officers being elected by the church
and reporting regularly to the church.

Section 2. Sunday School

There shall be a Sunday School, divided into departments and classes for all ages and conducted under the direction of the Sunday School director for the
study of God's Word.

The tasks of the Sunday School shall be to teach the
biblical revelation; reach persons for Christ and
church membership; perform the functions of the
church within its constituency; provide and interpret
information regarding the work of the church and
denomination.

Section 3. Training Union

There shall be a Training Union, divided into departments for all ages and conducted under the direction of a general director. The Training Union shall serve as the training organization of the church.

The tasks of the Training Union shall be to orient new church members; train church members to perform the functions of the church; train church leaders; teach Christian theology, Christian ethics, Christian history, and church polity and organization; provide and interpret information regarding the work of the church and denomination.

Section 4. Woman's Missionary Union

There shall be a Woman's Missionary Union with such officers and organization as needed. The tasks of the Woman's Missionary Union shall be to teach missions; engage in mission action; support world missions through praying and giving; provide and interpret information regarding the work of the church and the denomination.

Section 5. Brotherhood

There shall be a Brotherhood with such organization as needed. This program shall be directed by a director who shall be elected by the church. The tasks are to teach missions; engage in mission action, support world missions through praying and giving; provide and interpret information regarding the work of the church and the denomination.

Section 6. Church Music Program

There shall be a Church Music program under the direction of the music director. Such officers and/or organizations shall be included as needed. The music tasks shall be to teach music; train persons to lead, sing, and play music; provide music in the church and community; provide and interpret information regarding the work of the church and denomination.

VI. Ordinances

Section 1.   Baptism

A person who receives Jesus Christ as Savior by personal faith; who professes him publicly at any worship service; and who indicates a commitment to follow Christ as Lord, shall be received for baptism.

1. Baptism shall be by immersion in water.
2. Baptism shall be administered by the pastor or whomever the church shall authorize. The deacons shall assist in the preparation for, and observance of, baptism.
3. Baptism shall be administered as an act of worship during any worship service.
4. A person professing Christ and failing to be baptized after a reasonable length of time shall be counseled by the pastor and/or staff and deacons. If negative interest is ascertained, he shall be deleted from those awaiting baptism.

Section 2.   The Lord's Supper

The Lord's Supper is a symbolic act of obedience whereby members of the church, through partaking of the bread and fruit of the vine, commemorate the death of Jesus Christ and anticipate his second coming.

1. The Lord's Supper shall be observed quarterly, preferably the first Sunday of the quarter, or as otherwise scheduled.

2. The Lord's Supper shall be observed in the morning or evening worship services, rotating between the two.

3. The pastor and deacons shall be responsible for the administration of the Lord's Supper.

4. The deacons shall be responsible for the physical preparations of the Lord's Supper.

VII. Church Meetings

Section 1.   Worship Services
The church shall meet regularly each Sunday morning, Sunday evening, and Wednesday evening for preaching, instruction, evangelism, and for the worship of Almighty God. These meetings will be open for the entire membership of the church and for all people and shall be conducted under the direction of the pastor.

Section 2.   Special Services
Revival services and any other church meetings which will be essential in the promotion of the objectives of the church shall be placed on the church calendar.

Section 3.   Regular Business Meetings
Regular business meetings shall be held monthly on a designated Wednesday night.

Section 4.   Special Business Meetings

A specially called business meeting may be held to consider special matters of significant nature. A one-week notice of the subject, date, time, and location must be given for the specially called business meeting unless extreme urgency renders such notice impracticable.

Section 5.   Quorum

The quorum consists of those who attend the business meeting, provided it is a stated meeting or one that has been properly called.

Section 6.   Parliamentary Rules

Robert's Rules of Order, Revised, is the authority for parliamentary rules of procedure for all business meetings of the church.

VIII. Church Finances

Section 1.   Budget

The stewardship committee, in consultation with the church council, shall prepare and submit to the church for approval an inclusive budget, indicating by items the amount needed and sought for all local and worldwide expenses.

It is understood that membership in this church involves financial obligation to support the church and its causes with regular, proportionate gifts. Each new member shall, therefore, be immediately approached by a representative of the church for a pledge to the church's unified budget; and at least annually, plans

shall be put into operation for securing a worthy subscription from each member of the church.

Section 2.   Accounting Procedures

All funds for any and all purposes shall pass through
the hands of the church treasurer, or financial secretary, and be properly recorded on the books of the
church. The officer(s) shall be bonded.

A system of accounting that will adequately provide
for the handling of all funds shall be the responsibility
of the stewardship committee.

Section 3.   Fiscal Year

The fiscal year of the church shall run concurrently
with the church year which begins on October 1 and
ends on September 30.

IX. Church Operations Manual

Section 1.   Organizational chart

An organizational chart shall be prepared which will
depict lines of responsibility in the administration of
the church. This chart shall be reviewed periodically
by a special long-range planning committee and shall
be revised as needed. A copy shall be included in the
church operations manual.

Section 2.   Policies and Procedures

Church policies and procedures shall be described
in the church operations manual. The manual shall be
kept in the church office and made available to any
member of the church. The manual shall be main-

tained by the church secretary. Changes in policies and procedures may be initiated by any church member or organization. Addition, revision, or deletion of church policies requires: (1) the recommendation of the church officer or organization (including committees) to whose areas of assignment the policy relates, (2) discussion by the church council, and (3) approval by the church. Procedures may be added, revised, or deleted by: (1) recommendation of the appropriate officer or group, (2) approval by the church council, and (3) approval of the church if deemed necessary by the church council.

X. Amendments

Changes in this constitution and bylaws may be made at any regular business meeting of the church, provided each amendment shall have been presented in writing at a previous meeting, and copies of the proposed amendment be furnished to each member present. Amendments to the constitution shall be by two-thirds vote of all members of the church present entitled to vote; amendments to the bylaws shall have a concurrence of a majority of the members present and voting.

8. PASTOR AND STAFF MEMBERS
Understanding Their Work

Pastor

The pastor is responsible to the church for leading the church to determine its mission and move toward the attainment of its mission. He proclaims the gospel and provides pastoral care for persons in the church and the community. He serves as an enabler to involve church members in the work of the church so that its divine mission can be achieved.

His responsibilities are listed below.

1. Proclaim the gospel and lead church members in the proclamation of the gospel in the church and community.

2. Care for persons and lead church members to care for persons in the church and the community.

3. Provide administrative leadership to guide the church in the attainment of its divine mission.

4. Provide leadership for congregational services, and lead in conducting the church ordinances (Lord's Supper and baptism).

5. Conduct wedding ceremonies and funeral services.

6. Work closely with the deacons in their training and performance in their work of proclamation, car-

85

ing, and building up of the church fellowship.

7. Serve as chairman of the church council and provide administrative leadership for the total church program.

8. Supervise church staff members according to plan of staff organization, and provide for staff training and development.

Minister of Education

The minister of education is responsible to the pastor for providing staff leadership to the entire church educational program. He serves as an enabler to program organization leaders in planning, conducting, and evaluating the church educational program.

These responsibilities may be as follows:

1. Provide staff leadership to enable the church educational program to establish and attain its objectives and goals.

2. Serve as resource person to all educational program leaders and to church committee chairmen.

3. Work with the church nominating committee to select, enlist, and train qualified leaders for the church program.

4. Lead special church projects of educational and training nature such as camps, retreats, and training courses.

5. Study church needs for educational curriculum, and counsel with church leaders regarding available curriculum.

6. Supervise the production of informational and public relations materials, such as church publications

and news releases.

7. Supervise appropriate church staff members, such as age-group directors, youth director, educational secretary, custodian.

8. Participate as a member of the church council.

Minister of Music

The minister of music is responsible to the pastor for assisting the Church Music program in planning and conducting a comprehensive music program. This responsibility may be divided as follows:

1. Guide music program leaders in planning and conducting a comprehensive music program.

2. Assist the pastor in planning congregational services of the church.

3. Train leaders for the church music program and assist music leaders in the performance of their music groups and individuals in the church.

4. Direct congregational singing, and direct music groups as needed.

5. Coordinate the performance schedules of music groups and individuals in the church.

6. Assist music program leaders in developing and conducting a music program plan of visitation and enlistment.

7. Work in cooperation with appropriate persons, including nominating committee in selecting, enlisting, training, and counseling with song leaders, accompanists, and other musicians who serve in church program organizations.

8. Counsel with church music leaders regarding

needs for acquiring music materials, supplies, instruments, and other musical equipment.

9. Participate as a member of the church council.

Director of Youth Work

The director of youth work is usually supervised by the minister of education and is responsible for working with church leaders of youth and staff members to develop a comprehensive youth program.

His responsibilities are listed below.

1. Counsel with church program organization leaders in the planning, conducting, and evaluation of a comprehensive youth program.

2. Counsel with church program organization leaders and nominating committee to aid in the enlistment of qualified youth workers.

3. Lead training opportunities for youth workers.

4. Counsel with youth and youth leaders in the planning and conducting of special projects, such as tours and retreats.

5. Counsel with youth leaders regarding curriculum, space, equipment, and educational methods.

6. Participate as a member of the church council.

Director of Preschool Work

The director of preschool work is usually supervised by the minister of education and is responsible for working with appropriate church leaders and staff members to develop a comprehensive preschool program along the following lines:

1. Counsel with church program organization lead-

ers in the planning, conducting, and evaluation of a comprehensive preschool program.

2. Counsel with church program organization leaders and nominating committee to aid in the enlistment of qualified preschool workers.

3. Lead training opportunities for preschool workers.

4. Counsel with preschool leaders in the planning and conducting of special projects.

5. Counsel with preschool workers regarding curriculum, space, equipment, and educational methods.

6. Participate as a member of the church council.

Director of Recreation

The director of recreation is responsible for leading the church to develop a comprehensive recreation program that reaches church members and persons in the community. His responsibilities are listed below.

1. Counsel with church program organization leaders in the planning, conducting, and evaluation of a comprehensive recreation program.

2. Coordinate and administer church recreational activities and recreational facilities.

3. Counsel with the nominating committee to locate and enlist qualified church recreation workers.

4. Lead training opportunities for church recreation workers.

5. Counsel with recreation workers regarding curriculum, space, equipment, and educational methods.

6. Maintain inventory and proper care for recreational equipment and supplies.

7. Represent the church in planning and conducting recreational activities that relate to other churches and groups.

8. Participate as a member of the church council.

Associate Pastor

The associate pastor is responsible to the pastor for assisting in the proclamation, pastoral care, and administration of the church.

His responsibilities may include:

1. Provide assistance to the pastor in all areas of work as requested.

2. Supervise and provide coordination for church visitation activities, and assist pastor in hospital visitation, as requested.

3. Counsel with members of the church and community regarding pastoral care needs, as requested.

4. Assist in the worship services, as requested.

5. Perform wedding ceremonies and funeral services, as requested.

6. Participate as a member of the church council.

Church Business Administrator

The church business administrator is responsible to the pastor for administering church business affairs, such as finances, maintenance, food services, and church office operation.

His responsibilities are listed below.

1. Lead in developing and conducting an effective church business operation.

2. Manage the church office operation, and supervise appropriate personnel.

3. Direct the church maintenance and food services operations.

4. Serve as purchasing agent for the church.

5. Counsel with church officers and committees regarding church business matters.

6. Counsel with the chairman of the stewardship campaign, and provide assistance in planning and conducting the annual financial campaign.

7. Provide counsel on legal and church business matters.

8. Participate as a member of the church council.

Financial Secretary

The financial secretary is responsible for preparation and maintenance of all church financial records and reports. Specifically, the job may include:

1. Maintain record of all receipts and disbursements.

2. Post individual offering records.

3. Reconcile monthly bank statements.

4. Prepare monthly financial report.

5. Prepare appropriate records and reports as required by government.

6. Maintain record of purchase orders, invoices, etc.

7. Prepare checks for approved expenditures.

8. Perform other responsibilities, as assigned.

Church Secretary

The church secretary is responsible for performing secretarial duties, such as:

1. Perform stenographic work.
2. Maintain church records and files.
3. Serve as receptionist and answer telephone.
4. Type stencils and operate duplicating equipment.
5. Maintain church mailing lists.
6. Maintain church calendar.
7. Perform other responsibilities, as assigned.

9. PASTOR SELECTION COMMITTEE
Selecting a Pastor

The selection of a new pastor is one of the most important decisions a church faces. Every effort should be made to approach this awesome responsibility in a prayerful and orderly fashion.

Below is the process a church takes in its search for a new pastor, guided always by the Holy Spirit.

Steps in Selecting a Pastor

1. *Elect a Pastor Selection Committee*

The pastor selection committee should be elected by the church to locate, interview, and recommend a qualified person to serve as pastor. This committee has been called the pulpit committee. Pulpit committee, however, emphasizes only a portion of the work performed by a pastor. Preaching from the pulpit is an important function of the pastor, but it is only a part of his total job. He also serves in such capacities as counselor, teacher, and administrator. The title "pastor selection committee" seems more accurate and appropriate.

A pastor selection committee should always be elected by the church. The procedure by which the committee is presented to the church for election dif-

fers from church to church. Some churches instruct
the personnel committee to assume this additional
responsibility for recommending a pastor whenever
the need arises. In most cases, additional qualified
persons are added to the committee to provide wider
representation. Other churches ask the nominating
committee to nominate members to serve on the pastor selection committee.

Careful study should be given to the choice of committee members. All committee members should have
earned the respect of fellow church members by their
demonstrated Christian maturity and involvement in
the life and work of the church. Special attention
should be given to securing a representation from the
various age groups and life-styles of the church members. Select persons who will be able to attend committee meetings and who will be free to travel to interview recommended persons.

Committee membership will vary according to actual need. Five to seven members seems to be the
usual number most churches choose. A small church
may, of course, find that three members can serve
adequately. A larger church may need nine or more
members on the committee.

As soon as the committee is elected, it should organize itself in order to begin its work immediately.
Usually, a chairman, associate chairman, and secretary
are chosen.

It is a wise procedure to set regular meeting dates
in the beginning to insure that work will proceed in
a regular and orderly fashion.

2. *Determine Qualifications Needed in a New Pastor*

The pastor selection committee should seek information from as many church members as possible regarding the kind of pastor needed. Before beginning a formal search, the committee should first prepare a list of qualifications desired in a new pastor. Such a list will serve as a guideline for evaluating specific persons. Seek out every occasion when church members can express their views. The church bulletin could be used to remind members to share their views with committee members. A special meeting might be held with youth groups to hear their viewpoints. Special groups such as deacons, women's groups, Sunday School departments, and prayer meetings might be visited and persons asked to share views about the kind of pastor needed.

The committee should next prepare a specific list of qualifications they will be looking for in all persons they interview. By seeking God's leadership and prayerfully reaching agreement on the type of pastor needed, the committee can greatly reduce the frustration of the assignment.

3. *Agree on Committee Procedures to Follow*

Make decisions regarding procedural matters prior to starting the search for God's man for your church. By establishing operating procedures early, the committee can save many hours of frustration later.

What types of procedural decisions should be made? Possible examples might be how prospects will be located and evaluated, a plan for receiving recommendations, agreement that committee will recommend only one person at a time.

4. *Decide Where to Locate Prospects*

Establish contact with a variety of information sources to secure names of prospective pastors. Seek information about qualified prospects from pastors, superintendents of missions, state and denominational staff members. Teachers and administrative staff members of Baptist colleges and seminaries are usually good resource persons.

5. *Develop Areas of Discussion with Prospective Pastor*

Each committee should early agree on various subject areas about which they will talk with a prospective pastor. They also ought to be able to speak with clarity to all questions a prospective pastor may ask.

Here are some of the questions committee members might desire to explore with a candidate.

What educational level attained? Health? Previous pastoral experience? When and where converted? Call to ministry? Family status? Personal attitude about church and denomination? Attitude about evangelism, religious education, missions, stewardship, doctrines? Method of working with church leaders and church staff? Attitude toward state Baptist convention and Southern Baptist Convention? Study habits? Administrative ability? Counseling interests? Ability to plan? Visitation? Relation to community?

6. *Prepare to Answer Questions from Prospective Pastor*

The pastor selection committee should gather ap-

propriate information about the church and its work
in order to answer any questions a prospective pastor
may ask. Secure a copy of the church history, church
budget, organization chart, and other information
about the church's past and present program. Gather
basic facts about salary and staff benefits, such as
retirement, medical coverage, vacation, and housing
allowance. Be prepared to discuss church long-range
plans, budget, staff, and facility needs.

A committee should seek to answer all questions
asked by a prospective pastor. It is far better for a
candidate to hear both favorable and unfavorable facts
from the committee than to learn that the committee
did not give him full information prior to his acceptance.

7. *Determine How to Evaluate Prospects*

Gather information about all qualified persons that
have been recommended. Check carefully their qualifications against the criteria that the committee established earlier. Do not be rushed into recommending
someone to the church. Secure data on a number of
different persons.

After careful study of the qualifications of each person, place these names in priority order. Seek to secure additional information regarding the first three
names appearing on the priority list.

Next, select the name of your first choice and visit
with him. Participate in one of the worship services
that he leads. Identify yourself and ask for an appoint-
ment so that you may talk further. All or part of the

pastor selection committee members may be present for this discussion.

If the committee is sufficiently impressed with the prospective pastor after this discussion, you may desire to invite him to visit with the committee privately at your church. This provides the candidate an opportunity to see the church building and talk more specifically about subjects he may wish to discuss.

It is best for both the pastor and the church to put major agreements in writing. Items for discussion would include such matters as housing, salary, moving expense, retirement program, conventions, vacation, absence for revivals and other engagements, and car expenses.

8. *Recommend the Committee's Choice to the Church*

When the committee is unanimous in their choice for a prospective new pastor, the committee is then ready to present a formal recommendation. Alert the church, according to church policy, that a name will be recommended to the church on a certain date. Since the selection of a pastor is such a significant decision, a vote should be taken when the largest number of members can be present. Many churches vote on a new pastor at the Sunday morning service.

Orient the New Pastor

A full week of orientation at the beginning of a new pastorate would prove helpful to both the new pastor and the church.

In one week of discussion with strategic church

leaders, information can be secured by the new pastor that would otherwise take from six months to a year to learn.

How do you go about setting up such an orientation? The pastor selection committee could recommend a special week of orientation to the congregation. The week should be scheduled soon after the new pastor arrives. The purpose of the week would be to review with the new pastor the total life and work of the church. Opportunity should be given the new pastor to ask questions and to suggest possibilities for future consideration.

Each night the new pastor would meet with the respective program organization directors and strategic department leaders to discuss present and future plans. In addition to the verbal reports, church leaders should provide the pastor a typed list of the respective organizational officers and leaders, along with an overview of program plans. These reports should be prepared on paper of uniform size and format for compilation by the pastor.

The schedule below might be followed.

- Sunday. Sermons by the new pastor. Following the Sunday night service a churchwide reception could be scheduled for the pastor and his family. Consider inviting special guests from other churches, as well as public school, civic, and communications media leaders.
- Monday night. Discussion with deacons, church council members, and church officers.
- Tuesday night. Discussion with leaders of mis-

sions programs (Woman's Missionary Union and Brotherhood).

- Wednesday. Discussion with Sunday School officers and teachers.
- Thursday. Discussion with Training Union officers and leaders.
- Friday. Discussion with Church Music officers and leaders.

10. DEACONS
Serving Pastoral Ministries

The prototype of today's deacon is found in the Acts 6 account of seven men being appointed by the Jerusalem church to resolve a fellowship problem. The word "deacon" does not appear in this scriptural account. Baptists generally agree, however, that these seven Christian men represent the beginning of a deacon ministry.

Christian fellowship was being threatened in the Jerusalem church as the Greek-speaking widows told how they felt they were being mistreated. Seven men were appointed to resolve the potential problem of broken fellowship that was threatening the early church.

The seven were obviously successful in resolving the problem because Acts 6:7 reports: "And the word of God increased; and the number of the disciples multiplied in Jerusalem greatly; and a great company of the priests were obedient to the faith."

High standards were set for the seven men who were chosen by the Jerusalem church. Paul later stressed equally significant qualifications for deacons in 1 Timothy 3:1–12 as he set forth the spiritual requirements for deacon. Paul said: "Let these also first be proved; then let them use the office of a deacon, being found blameless" (1 Tim. 3:10).

The word "deacon" is from the Greek word *diakonos* which means servant. As a servant of Christ, a deacon serves in whatever areas of need a church assigns. It was only a few years after the events recorded in Acts 6 that the word "deacon" came to designate a more formal church office. In Philippians 1:1, for example, Paul mentions deacons in his salutation "Paul and Timotheus, the servants of Jesus Christ, to all the saints in Christ Jesus which are at Philippi, with the bishops and deacons." Within a few years the office of deacon had developed. By A.D. 250 the office of deacon was being considered a formal part of the clergy.

It was not until the Reformation that the deacon was again spoken of as a layman. John Calvin began to preach and write about the deacon as a lay minister. Calvin stressed that the work of the deacon was a lay ministry of preaching and service to the sick and needy.

During the 1700's the deacon in America played a significant role. He was often the one who provided spiritual leadership to members of a congregation when inclement weather kept the part-time pastor from reaching the church community. Deacons have had a rich heritage of service through the centuries in America.

Gradually deacons were called on to handle more of the administrative work of the church. Oftentimes the deacons were the only elected church officers available to care for finances and property. Through the years the unfortunate phrase "board of deacons" developed. The concept of a legislative board of any kind is completely foreign to congregational church polity. Only the congregation, under the leadership of the Holy Spirit, should make major decisions for a church.

As employed church staffs have enlarged and church program organizations have expanded, churches are again examining the work of the deacon. Church committees are now responsible for much of the church's administrative work, such as budgets, property maintenance, and church personnel matters.

Responsibilities of Deacons

In a large number of churches today, deacons are serving in the area of pastoral ministries. In such a ministry they perform the work that is listed below.

1. *Proclaim the Gospel to Believers and Unbelievers*

   - Personal witnessing activities
   - Preaching as a layman
   - Church revival support

2. *Care for the Church's Members and Other Persons in the Community*

   - Ministering in times of crisis
   - Listening to burdened persons
   - Referring persons in need to qualified sources for assistance
   - Counseling on vocational guidance and family ministry

3. *Build Christian Fellowship Among Church Members*

- Sharing information about the church's life and work
- Assisting in administering ordinances

4. *Serve as an Exemplar Christian Leader*

- Set an example in Christian life
- Provide personal support to church activities

In these areas of need, deacons stand alongside their pastors as colaborers in a spiritual ministry. For additional information about the work of the deacon, see *The Ministry of the Deacon* by Howard B. Foshee and the quarterly magazine *The Deacon*. Both resources are published by the Sunday School Board, Nashville, Tennessee.

Deacon Election

There are many different plans followed by churches in electing deacons. Two basic approaches are predominant with variations of these two primary plans.

1. *Deacons Selected by the Congregation*

Acts 6 gives good insight for churches in selecting deacons. The apostles called the congregation together and said: "Wherefore, brethren, look ye out among you seven men of honest report, full of the Holy Ghost and wisdom, whom we may appoint over this business" (v. 3). The entire congregation had a voice in selecting and electing the seven.

A list composed of every adult male church member

is prepared. The list does not contain the names of deacons now serving or the names of persons who have requested that their names be omitted. These name are presented as a ballot at a Sunday morning worship service. The scriptural qualifications of deacons are read. A review of the church's deacon ministry is reviewed for the congregation. The need for spiritually qualified deacons is stressed. Church members are given a ballot and asked to check the required number of names.

A committee of deacons counts the deacon ballots and presents the results to the chairman of deacons. The chairman of deacons and the pastor then visit persons receiving the highest number of votes. They discuss the qualifications of deacons and the expectations that the church holds for each deacon. The man is not told how many votes he received or where his name appears on the list. Following this discussion, the decision is made by the man as to whether he will serve as a deacon. If an individual decides not to serve, the chairman of deacons and pastor go to the person who received the next largest number of votes. This procedure is continued until the required number of deacons is secured.

2. *Deacons Selected by Nominating Committee*

There are some churches that select deacons for congregational approval in the same manner as other church leaders are recommended. This approach to selection is through the church nominating committee.

The church nominating committee first studies the qualifications and special requirements that the church follows for deacon selection. The church membership role is then studied carefully to find persons who qualify.

Some nominating committees seek out recommendations from church members. Church members are requested to share names of prospective deacon candidates with the nominating committee.

After a list of names has been compiled, each prospective deacon is visited by the pastor, chairman of deacons, and chairman of the nominating committee. At this meeting, the spiritual qualifications and other church expectations for deacons are discussed. A person may withdraw his name if he desires to do so following this interview. The final list of names is presented to the church as a recommendation from the church nominating committee.

Deacon Family Ministry Plan

The Deacon Family Ministry Plan is a way by which deacons minister to every church family through a planned visitation program. The Deacon Family Ministry Plan is not just a special project but a plan by which the spiritual ministry of deacons is carried out.

The chairman of deacons leads in organizing the deacons to serve church families. Approximately twelve to fifteen church families are assigned to each deacon who is then responsible for maintaining regular contact with each church family member.

The Deacon Family Ministry Plan offers unlimited

opportunities to each deacon for performing his work of proclaiming the gospel to believers and unbelievers, caring for church members and other persons of the community, building and maintaining Christian fellowship, and being an exemplar Christian leader.

The deacon chairman is responsible for organizing the entire church membership by families. He assigns to each deacon a proportionate number of families. The deacon chairman also works with the pastor and Church Training director to develop an annual deacon training program. Many deacon chairmen set aside a portion of each deacons meeting for training deacons in the skills necessary for serving more effectively.

The chairman also is responsible for keeping deacons well informed and highly motivated. He calls for regular reports from each deacon on his family list. Deacons' meetings can provide moments of genuine worship as deacons report their experiences during the past month. Time for sharing victories, celebrating Christian fellowship, and praying for special needs of specific persons or families should be provided for each deacon meeting.

Families can be assigned alphabetically to deacons in churches that serve a limited geographical community. Other churches that minister to an entire city or region may find it best to assign church families by geographical zones so that deacons can minister to families in a small area. If possible, it is best to assign families to deacons who live in the same community as the deacon.

Some deacons are asked to keep the same list of families for his full term of service. The chief value of this plan is that each deacon has adequate time to learn the needs of every person in his group. Other churches ask deacons to serve a specific group of families for only one year. This procedure allows deacons to know and serve a larger number of family members during their deacon terms.

When deacons reach a place in their work where additional officers are needed, they may add a proclamation leader, care leader, fellowship leader, and a community relations leader.

Each of these additional deacon officers is responsible for correlating his area of specialized work. For example, when the deacons decide to carry out a project relating to church fellowship improvement, the deacon fellowship leader provides leadership for this project. In addition, throughout the year the deacon fellowship leader is responsible for discovering additional needs in the church for fellowship, encouraging the deacons to be alert to fellowship problems, providing deacon training to increase skills in fellowship development, and reporting on deacon achievements in fellowship development.

Additional resources are contained in the quarterly magazine *The Deacon,* and the Program Help pamphlet "The Deacon Family Ministry Plan." Both resources are available from the Sunday School Board of the Southern Baptist Convention, Nashville, Tennessee.

11. CHURCH COMMITTEES AND CHURCH OFFICERS
Understanding Their Work

Churches perform much of their administrative service type work through church committees and church officers. Both church committees and church officers are responsible for assisting the congregation to handle administrative matters such as finances, facilities, and personnel. A church committee is composed of a limited number of persons who are charged with performing a specific job for the church. Experience has proved that a committee can study and implement a specialized assignment more efficiently than can the entire church membership.

Church Committees

Church committee members are usually nominated by the church nominating committee and elected by the church. Since the church brings each church committee into existence, each committee reports back to the church. There should be a regular time allocated at each church business meeting for church committees to report on work accomplished.

Membership of church committees should be limited to as few members as necessary. Five to seven committee members are usually adequate. In small churches, committees should be limited to three persons. Each committee can, of course, secure resource persons to provide specialized information that relates to the problem under consideration. These temporary resource persons do not have voting privileges and do not become members of the committee.

Rotation of committee membership is becoming a standard practice in churches. Committee membership is usually for a three-year period. Rotation insures that a committee keeps two thirds of its experienced members and rotates one third of its members. To maintain a functioning rotation plan, a rotating committee member should be required to wait one year before being returned to a committee.

1. *Nominating Committee*

The basic responsibility of the church nominating committee is to locate, screen, and recommend to the church qualified persons to fill all church-elected positions requiring volunteer leaders. The committee is usually elected by the church for a three-year term of office. With one third of the committee members rotating off each year, opportunity is provided for the remaining members to recommend proposed new members for the church nominating committee. Members of the church council (leaders of church program organizations) may meet with the nominating committee as desired.

The duties of the nominating committee are:

1. Locate, interview, screen, and recommend qualified persons for all church positions requiring volunteers (church program organization leaders, church

program service leaders, church committee members, and general church officers).

2. Counsel with church leaders regarding need for volunteer workers and the performance of present volunteer workers.

3. Develop and operate by a plan that distributes leadership according to priority needs.

4. Nominate qualified members for special church committees approved by the church during the year.

5. Present names of recommended workers to the church for approval.

2. *Property and Space Committee*

The property and space committee is responsible for the care of all church property and buildings. It also makes studies and recommendations regarding need for additional space and furnishings for church program organizations.

The duties of the property and space committee are listed below.

1. Make regular inspection of all church property and keep current inventory of all furnishings and equipment. Recommend policies regarding use of church property and furnishings.

2. Make annual study of space needs and allocation to determine if adjustment is needed. Recommend additional space if needed for growth.

3. Work with missions committee to secure and adequately maintain property for mission use.

4. Work with the church personnel committee in securing and training new maintenance personnel.

5. Develop and make recommendations regarding maintenance policies and procedures.

6. Develop and make recommendations regarding adequate insurance on all buildings, equipment, and furnishings.

7. Develop recommendations regarding annual budget needs and administer maintenance budget.

3. *Stewardship Committee*

The stewardship committee is responsible to the church for stewardship planning, stewardship promotion, and administration of church finances according to church financial policies. Its members are recommended to the church by the nominating committee and elected by the church. Members usually serve for three years.

The duties of the stewardship committee are:

1. Develop and recommend to the church council an overall stewardship information plan.

2. Develop and recommend a church budget to the church.

3. Plan and direct the church's budget subscription plan.

4. Conduct studies and make recommendations to the church concerning proposed expenditures not included in the budget.

5. Review expenditures periodically in terms of budget allocations and recommend adjustments to the church as necessary.

6. Develop and recommend to the church financial policies and procedures.

4. *Personnel Committee*

The major concern of this committee is for locating, interviewing, and recommending qualified persons for all employed church staff positions. A church may add additional persons temporarily to the committee for broader representation when seeking a new pastor. The term of office for members is usually three years.

The duties of the personnel committee are:

1. Make studies regarding the need for additional staff personnel.

2. Develop and keep current all position descriptions for staff personnel.

3. Develop and keep current an organization chart and manual of policies and procedures regarding all staff personnel.

4. Locate, interview, and recommend to the church all employed staff personnel. Large churches may delegate the employment of clerical and maintenance personnel to the appropriate supervisor according to established church policy.

5. Prepare and recommend to the church a salary and staff benefit plan. Keep plan current.

6. Prepare and recommend to the church policies and procedures relating to church staff. Keep policies and procedures current.

5. *Missions Committee*

The work of the missions committee is to make studies, recommend plans, and administer work as assigned by the church. Term of office is usually three years. Membership is recommended to the church by the nominating committee.

The duties of the missions committee are:

1. Conduct studies and recommend plans for local mission work.

2. Work through the church council as the council coordinates the mission work of the church.

3. Establish and maintain communication with the associational missions committee and other appropriate groups outside the church.

4. Request and administer resources, according to the church's policy and procedure, for the work assigned to it.

6. *History Committee*

Gathering and preserving historical records pertaining to the work of the church is the chief responsibility of the history committee. The term of office is usually three years, and members are recommended to the church by the nominating committee.

The duties of the history committee are:

1. Gather and preserve all significant church records. Work closely with the church clerk in acquiring and maintaining church records for archival purposes.

2. Prepare or update church history at regular intervals.

3. Recommend policies and procedures regarding historical records.

4. Seek ways to educate and inspire church members through the use of church history information.

7. *Public Relations Committee*

The public relations committee is charged with the responsibility to communicate the church's mission and work to members of the church and to the community. Members are recommended by the nominating committee to the church usually for a three-year term.

The duties of the public relations committee are listed below.

1. Assist church leaders to communicate the message of the church to publics within and without the church.

2. Make studies and recommendations regarding the need for church use of appropriate media to reach specific target audiences.

3. Assist the church member to better understand the value of good church public relations and how the member can improve relations for the church.

4. Recommend appropriate policies and projects to improve church public relations.

8. *Food Services Committee*

The committee is responsible for securing more effective food services. Members are recommended by the nominating committee usually for a term of three years.

The duties of the food services committee are listed below.

1. Make studies regarding the food services needed by the church.

2. Recommend food services needed by the church.

3. Work with the personnel committee in securing and training food services personnel.

4. Prepare and recommend policies regarding food services.

5. Prepare and recommend proposed food services budget to budget preparation committee. Administer approved food services budget.

9. *Ushers Committee*

Ushers are to assist leaders and participants before, during, and following worship and special congregational services. The chairman of ushers is recommended by the nominating committee and usually serves for three years. He usually is responsible for selecting ushers as needed. Some churches elect all ushers.

The duties of the ushers committee are listed below.

1. Greet and seat persons appropriately at worship and other congregational services.

2. Provide information and assistance to persons attending as needed.

3. Work closely with pastor or leader of congregational service to assist as needed.

4. Make certain that the auditorium is orderly before and after the service in order to enhance the spirit of worship.

5. Assist in receiving offering as required.

10. *Pastor Selection Committee (Pulpit)*

The pastor selection committee is a special committee rather than a standing committee that functions at all times. As a special committee it functions until its special assignment is completed. The chief responsibility of the pastor selection committee is to determine the characteristics of a proposed pastor desired by the church members, seek out possible prospects, interview prospects, and prayerfully recommend a qualified person to the church.

The church personnel committee, plus additional persons selected to achieve a wider representation, may make up the membership of the pastor selection committee. Members usually are recommended to the church by the nominating committee.

The duties of the pastor selection committee are listed below.

1. Establish profile of characteristics desired in a new pastor.

2. Secure information about prospective pastors.

3. Investigate prospects to determine if they meet established characteristics desired.

4. Interview choice for prospective pastor. (Contact only one person at a time.)

5. Invite prospect to visit the church. Make plans for his visit.

6. Recommend that church issue "call" to committee-approved prospect.

7. Contact prospect to notify him of action by church. (In case church does not approve the committee's recommendation, contact prospect immediately and tell him of church action.)

8. Make arrangements for moving new pastor to church field.

9. Make arrangements for pastors to get started well in the church and community.

11. *Long-Range Planning Committee*

The chief work of the long-range planning committee is to study long-range church and community needs, analyze the present effectiveness of the church's work, set long-range objectives, goals, and strategies. This committee is usually a special committee recommended to the church by the nominating committee.

The duties of the long-range planning committee are listed below.

1. Analyze present and future needs of the church and community.

2. Set church objectives, goals, and strategies.

3. Maintain communication with church members throughout the planning process.

4. Present specific long-range plans to church for study and approval.

12. *Building Committee*

The building committee implements the building plans that result from the study and analysis made by the survey and planning committee. (The survey and planning committee precedes the building committee and is responsible for analyzing present and future program needs, deciding on what building, space, and property is going to be required.)

The duties of the building committee are:

1. Study recommendations made by the survey and

planning committee.

2. Prepare a building calendar. Maintain communication with church members.

3. Employ an architect.

4. Secure counsel from Church Architecture Department, Sunday School Board. Counsel with architect.

5. Place bids and award contracts.

6. Prepare budget for new building to be constructed.

7. Analyze bills relating to building program and process for payment.

8. Accept building when completion is approved by architect and building committee.

Church Officers

There are certain administrative service type jobs required in most churches that are best performed by individuals who possess specific skills. Church officers are nominated by the nominating committee and elected by the church.

1. *Moderator*

The chief responsibility of the moderator is to make preparation and to preside at the church business meetings.

The moderator is often recommended by the church nominating committee and elected by the church. The term of office is usually for three years. Many churches elect the pastor to serve as moderator.

The duties of the moderator are:

1. Preside at church business meetings.
2. Announce special church business meetings.
3. Develop church business meeting agenda in cooperation with appropriate persons.
4. Serve as resource to church clerk in preparation of church business meeting minutes.

2. *Church Clerk*

The church clerk has responsibility for keeping accurate records of all church business transactions approved in church business meetings. The clerk is nominated by the church nominating committee and the term of office is usually for three years.

The duties of the church clerk are listed below.

1. Record and maintain all actions taken by the church in business session.
2. Prepare and submit to the church records for the annual church letter to the association, and submit letter to association after church approval.
3. Prepare and mail all official church correspondence.
4. Work with moderator in preparation of agenda for church business meeting.
5. Serve as resource person to church history committee as requested.

3. *Treasurer*

The church treasurer is responsible for proper receipt, accounting, and disbursement of church funds within proper policies established by the church for adequate financial control.

The treasurer is nominated by the church nominating committee and elected by the church. The term of office is usually for three years. Some churches provide various assistants to the treasurer as needed.

The duties of the treasurer are listed below.

1. Work closely with the church stewardship committee to recommend and/or implement approved church policies relating to church finances.

2. Keep accurate records of all monies received and disbursed.

3. Work closely with the approved person who records each member's contributions and mails report quarterly to member.

4. Check supporting data for all check requests prior to issuing check for approved cosigner.

5. Prepare monthly reports to the church stewardship committee and to the church.

6. Submit accurate financial records for annual audit according to church policy.

4. *Trustees*

The church trustees serve as legal representatives for the church according to instructions from the church in business session. They are recommended by the church. The term of office is usually three years.

The duties of trustees are:

1. Act as legal agents for the church.

2. Maintain all church legal documents for safekeeping.

12. CHURCH COUNCIL
Planning Total Church Program

Through experience, churches have discovered that strategic church-elected leaders and church staff members need to meet at regular intervals to plan, coordinate, and evaluate the total church program. In many Baptist churches this planning group is called the church council. The pastor usually serves as chairman of the church council.

Church Council

The church council membership is usually composed of church leaders who have been elected to direct church program organizations and other support groups such as church library and strategic committees. As church council members, these leaders are responsible for thinking in terms of the total church program rather than just the welfare of the organization they lead.

Each church needs to determine its long-range objectives, short-range goals, and basic strategies for achieving these objectives and goals. The church council does the staff work of planning, coordinating, and evaluating the total church program. A church does not relinquish its responsibility for final approval after the church council makes its recommendations.

The work of the church council is both advisory and correlating. It serves as the channel through which various church organizations, church committees, and church staff members coordinate work into a total church program. Care should always be taken to keep a church council from becoming an administrative or legislative group. Actual implementation plans should be carried out by appropriate church organizations or committees.

1. Work of the Church Council

A description of the church council's primary work includes the areas listed below.

1. Develop and recommend to the congregation suggested church objectives and goals.

Each church needs to develop its own statement of purpose or mission. Members should be led to consider the spiritual foundations upon which their church is built. Churches should seek to understand the kind of a spiritual organism they want to become under the leadership of God. Only with a knowledge of long-range objectives, short-range goals, and strategic approaches for achieving its priority work can a congregation continue to grow.

2. Develop and recommend to the congregation strategies for reaching church goals.

Goals do not achieve themselves. Strategic approaches for attaining goals must be set. Church organizations contribute in their distinctive ways to the attainment of a church's total goals. By moving as a team toward the attainment of church goals, church organizations can thereby synchronize their energy and help the entire church move toward its priority goals.

3. Study, analyze, and coordinate suggested program plans from individual church council members to synchronize and harmonize suggested programs of work. Discussion of these suggested plans will provide a better understanding and support by all church council members. Team spirit develops only when every person knows, understands, appreciates, and depends on the unique contributions of other members of the team.

4. Present the proposed church program plans for the coming year to the congregation for approval.

All plans proposed by the church council should help the church move toward the attainment of its objectives and goals. Activity for activity's sake should be discouraged. Church resources, such as time, leaders, facilities, and budget should always be allocated to priority plans. A church council helps a church determine its priorities.

5. Study and analyze program achievements in terms of the church goals and objectives. Make periodic reports to the church membership.

Since the church council members are elected by the church, the church council reports to the church at regular intervals. All major program proposals should be reported to the church for discussion and approval.

2. *Duties of Church Council Chairman*

The pastor usually serves as chairman of the church council. The suggested duties of the church council chairman are listed below.

1. Prepare agenda for church council meetings.

2. Preside at church council meetings.

3. Lead church council members to develop church objectives, short-range goals, and strategies for attaining priorities.

4. Present total church program plans to the congregation for approval.

5. Develop plans for training church council members to perform effectively.

6. Make certain that church council minutes are maintained and distributed on schedule.

How to Plan and Launch the Church Program

A growing church does not just happen. There is a direct relationship between the quality of preparation and the results.

Enlistment of workers should start early. Workers need training to prepare for their new jobs. Planning is required if priorities are to be set. Work should be coordinated to insure proper support. The required work cannot be done in preparation for the new church year unless it is started early.

The following schedule has proved effective for many churches as they have prepared for the new year's work. Assuming that the new church year begins October 1, this plan calls for preparation work to begin the preceding February. By following a systematic schedule, a church can carefully elect and train its workers, plan the new year's work, and enthusiastically launch the new program.

1. *Elect church nominating committee*   *February*

Church nominating committee members should be elected in February in order to begin their work early in preparation for the new church year, which will begin the following October 1.

2. *Elect directors of church program organizations*   *March*

Directors of church program organizations should be elected first so that they can participate in the selection of other leaders in their program organization. Planning processes can also be started if church program organization directors are elected early.

3. *Train church council members*   *April*

The church council is composed of directors of church program organizations and other strategic church leaders. The church council is the planning group that has responsibility for planning, coordinating, and evaluating the total church program. Council members need to be trained early so that they can begin their work of discovering specific needs, establishing priorities, and setting church goals.

4. *Start church council planning*   *April*

By the month of May, the church council should begin planning the total church program for the new church year. Planning involves establishing priorities, setting goals and strategies, and establishing specific projects.

5. *Elect and train church organization leaders*   *May*

By the month of May, the church program organization leaders should be elected so that they can begin their work early in preparation for the new church year. Training should also be provided church program organization leaders so they can serve more effectively.

6. *Start organization planning* *June*

After church program organization leaders are elected, actual planning should be begun to allow church program organizations to support church goals. If planning can be begun by early June, adequate time will be available for planning a total church program.

7. *Elect and train church program organization workers and church committee members* *June*

By June, all workers in church program organizations as well as church committee members should be elected and trained. Early election and training of workers provide additional time for them to make preparation for the new church year.

8. *Launch total church program* *September*

After the church program has been planned, all efforts should be focused on launching the program for the new church year. Priority goals and special projects should be interpreted. Celebration by the church is most appropriate when a church program has been developed and launched for the new church year.

13. CHURCH RECORDS
Membership and Financial

Accurate church records are essential to a growing church. Records provide information about persons who need to be reached for Christ and church membership. Records are essential to building a program of education, training, and Christian nurture. Records are required if adequate goal-planning is to be achieved. Records are essential ingredients if any kind of evaluation is to be done after projects are completed to determine if goals were attained.

Records can easily be established and maintained in a church if there is sufficient desire. The record system can be elaborate and housed in expensive equipment. On the other hand, adequate records can be kept in a shoe box.

Several features should characterize a membership record system. It should be (1) simple, (2) centralized, (3) accessible, (4) flexible.

The following membership record system seeks to combine these qualities. The record forms are available in Baptist Book Stores.

Membership Records

The Master Membership Record is a 4 by 6 multipurpose form that serves as the basic record for building a comprehensive church record system. The record contains space for collecting maximum information about both church members and members of church program organizations. Listed alphabetically, the record provides a flexible plan for maintaining information about all persons who participate in the life and work of the church. The use of the Master Membership Record eliminates the need for keeping

CM | CHR | OB | OD | U | SS | TU | MM | WMU | BH | T | P | M | F

NAME _____ Residence _____

BIRTHDATE: Month _____ Day _____ Year _____ Phone _____

Christian? _____ Date Profession Made _____ Date Joined _____

Joined by _____ Date Baptized _____ Letter Received _____

Letter from _____ Membership No. _____

Dismissed _____ Dismissal No. _____

If member another church, what church? _____

SUNDAY SCHOOL: Date Enrolled _____ Dept. _____ Class _____

               Date Dropped _____ Reason _____

TRAINING UNION: Date Enrolled _____ Dept. _____ Union _____

              Date Dropped _____ Reason _____

MUSIC MINISTRY: Choir _____ Voice _____ Instrument _____ Song Ldr. _____

W.M.U.: Circle _____ Aux _____ B.Bhd. Member _____ R.A. _____

CHURCH ACTIVITY: Worker in S.S. _____ ; T.U. _____ ; W.M.U _____

Deacon _____ ; Tither _____ ; Current Pledge:Yes __; No __; Miscellaneous _____

Business _____ Phone _____

Residence _____ Phone _____

NAME   CM | CHR | OB | OD | U | SS | TU | MM | WMU | BH | T | P | M | F

MASTER MEMBERSHIP RECORD
Code 4384-04, MCE, Broadman Supplies, Nashville, Tenn. Prt'd in USA.

several different record systems because it shows the member's participation in various church program organizations.

The Master Membership Record is filled out when a person first joins the church or a church program organization. Information is usually transferred to the Master Membership Record from the Registration Record or the Church Membership and Decision Record. Once the Master Membership Record is completed, it is not necessary to fill out another church or church program organization record when a person joins another program organization. Basic information about each person is already in the church office on the Master Membership Record, so the record is simply updated with the new information.

Master Membership Record cards are maintained in alphabetical order. They may be kept in either a vertical file drawer or in a visible file cabinet. When records are kept in a visible file, changes can be made without taking the record form from the file by checking the appropriate code at the bottom of the record form.

It is best to type in permanent information, such as name, birthdate, and other basic information, and to use a pencil for writing information that is subject to frequent change.

The following code identifications are available

CM—Church member

CHR—Christian, not a church member

OB—Member other Baptist church

OD—Member other denomination

U—Unsaved, evangelism prospect

SS—Member of Sunday School

TU—Member of Training Union

MM—Music Ministry

WMU—Member WMU or auxiliary

BH—Member of Brotherhood or RA

P—Has made current pledge

T—Is a tither

M—Male

F—Female

CHRONOLOGICAL MEMBERSHIP ROLL

Page _____

This is the permanent church roll for *Historical Record.* Use permanent ink or typewriter. The number on roll may be determined at any time by taking the last number listed in Membership Number column and subtracting the last number in Dismissal Number column. To indicate the end of the associational year, draw a line in colored ink or pencil at the proper space and enter totals in the color chosen.

An alphabetical roll should be kept for the *Working Record.* Master Membership Record Card MC4 is suggested.

MEMBERSHIP NUMBER	HOW RECEIVED					DATE RECEIVED OR DISMISSED	NAME (Use reverse side if additional information desired.)	HOW DISMISSED					DISMISSAL NUMBER
	BAPTISM	LETTER	STATEMENT	RESTORATION				DEATH	LETTER	ERASURE	EXCLUSION		

The Chronological Membership Roll record provides a permanent church roll for both current and historical purposes. Information should be recorded on the form with a typewriter or permanent ink.

A basic value of the Chronological Membership Roll is that information is maintained by chronological sequence date and shows when a member has been added or removed from the church roll. The record serves primarily as a permanent historical record of church membership while the Master Membership Record serves as a daily operational file.

The Chronological Membership Roll lists alphabetically all names on the church roll. There are columns for keeping appropriate information such as how received, how dismissed, date received, date dismissed. In addition, a membership number and a dismissal number are recorded. As each new member is added to the record, a chronological number is assigned. When a church member moves to another church or dies, a chronological dismissal number is assigned. The exact number of church members can

---

REGISTRATION RECORD

Form 1 Fill out in triplicate

Check one: ☐ Visitor   ☐ New Member

Organization (S.S., T.U., C.M., etc.)	Department	Class/group/choir/etc.	Date

Visitor or New Member

Name			Home phone no.
Street address	City	State	Zip Code
Mailing address (if different)		Date of birth	School grade
Church member? ☐ Yes ☐ No	Church to which you belong		City

New member only

Business address		Business phone no.
Parents' name (if you live with parents)	Are your parents church members? Father: ☐ Yes ☐ No Mother: ☐ Yes ☐ No	
Church to which Father belongs City	Church to which Mother belongs	City

Office

New member assigned to:

Class/group/choir   Dept.

Send original to general secretary, copy to department, copy to class/group/choir
Code 4380-01, Broadman Supplies, Nashville, Tenn., Printed in U.S.A.

be determined at any date by subtracting the last number in the Dismissal (Decrease) column from the Membership (Received) column.

The Registration Record is a triplicate record form used for registering both new members and visitors in Sunday School and Training Union. Appropriate information should be recorded by the organization classification officer or secretary. The original record copy goes to the general secretary of a specific church program organization. The duplicate copy is forwarded to the department secretary and the triplicate copy is used by the class outreach leader.

The Church Membership and Decision Record contains information regarding any decision that a person may make in a worship service. This 4 by 6 triplicate carbon record form is flexible enough to secure information about any kind of decision that is made.

CHURCH MEMBERSHIP AND DECISION RECORD

MR.
MRS
MISS _____ DATE _____

RESIDENCE _____ PHONE _____

MAILING ADDRESS (IF DIFFERENT) _____

BUSINESS ADDRESS _____ PHONE _____

      BIRTHDATE: MONTH _____ DAY _____ YEAR _____
NAME AND ADDRESS OF NEAREST OF KIN OTHER THAN ABOVE ADDRESS
_____
_____

MAKES THE FOLLOWING PUBLIC COMMITMENT:

( ) ACCEPTS CHRIST AS PERSONAL SAVIOUR AND LORD

( ) DESIRES MEMBERSHIP IN THIS CHURCH BY BAPTISM _____ BY STATEMENT _____

( ) BY LETTER FROM _____
     ADDRESS OF CHURCH

( ) DEDICATES LIFE FOR CHURCH RELATED VOCATION _____
                                    (AREA IF KNOWN)

( ) REDEDICATES LIFE TO CHRIST

( ) OTHER DECISION _____
        CODE 4384 06, ACM 6, BROADMAN SUPPLIES, NASHVILLE, TENNESSEE, PRINTED IN U.S.A

The original white copy is used by the church clerk or church secretary to transfer appropriate information to the Master Membership Record and Chronological Membership Roll. The duplicate blue copy usually goes to the pastor for his use in follow-up. The triplicate pink copy is available for different purposes. It may be used by the deacon who is assigned the new church member, or it may be placed in the visitation file of a Sunday School department or class.

APPLICATION FOR CHURCH MEMBERSHIP

MR.
MRS.
MISS. _____ DATE _____

RESIDENCE_____ PHONE_____

MAILING ADDRESS (IF DIFFERENT) _____

BUSINESS ADDRESS _____ PHONE _____

    BIRTHDATE: MONTH _____ DAY_____ YEAR_____

NAME AND ADDRESS OF NEAREST OF KIN OTHER THAN ABOVE ADDRESS

MAKES THE FOLLOWING PUBLIC COMMITMENT:

( ) ACCEPTS CHRIST AS PERSONAL SAVIOUR AND LORD.

( ) DESIRES MEMBERSHIP IN THIS CHURCH: BY BAPTISM_____; BY STATEMENT_____;

( ) BY LETTER FROM_____

    ADDRESS OF CHURCH _____

( ) DEDICATES LIFE FOR CHURCH RELATED VOCATION _____
                                    (AREA IF KNOWN)

( ) REDEDICATES LIFE TO CHRIST.

( ) OTHER DECISION _____

FOR CLERK'S USE ONLY
DATE
BAPTIZED_____
DATE
LETTER REC'D._____

Code 4384-05, ACM-5, Broadman Supplies, Nashville, Tennessee, Printed in U.S.A.

The application for Church Membership record form is a 4 by 6 alternate record that may be used in place of the triple carbon Church Membership and Decision Card. It is maintained as a permanent record in a vertical file. This record form provides space for recording most decisions that persons may make in a worship service.

REQUEST FOR CHURCH LETTER

To the clerk of _____ Church

of _____

(NAME OF TOWN AND STATE)

_____

(NAME OF MEMBER)

has united with our church on the promise of a letter from your church. After proper action
by your church, please forward the letter with the Training and other Service records to us.

_____ Church

_____

(STREET AND NUMBER)   (P. O. BOX)

_____   _____   _____

(TOWN)   (STATE)   (ZIP)

Date _____   _____ Church Clerk

CODE 4384-11. FORM RCS BROADMAN SUPPLIES, NASHVILLE, TENNESSEE. PRINTED IN U. S. A.

The Request for Church Letter is a 4 by 6 duplicate
carbon form that is used by the church clerk to request
a church letter from another church. The original top
card may be sent through the mail as a postal card.
The duplicate record is kept by the church clerk until
the requested church letter is received. After the
church letter is received by the requesting church, the
date of receipt is recorded on the Chronological Membership Roll.

The Letter of Transfer is used by the church clerk
to transfer a church letter to another church after official approval has been voted in business session. This
4 by 6 record card may be used as a postal card. After
the requested church letter is mailed, the name of the
dismissed member and the dismissal date should be
recorded on the Chronological Membership Roll. The
Master Membership Record of the dismissed member

LETTER OF TRANSFER

To the _____ Church

_____
(Street and Number — P. O. Box)   (Town and State)

THIS IS TO CERTIFY, That _____
is a member of this church in regular standing, and, in compliance with
request is given this letter of transfer. We list below the record of Service:

_____

_____

Training Certificates will be sent under separate cover.

By order of the church _____ 19 _____

_____ Church Clerk

_____ Church

_____
                        Town   State
CODE 4384-12
            BROADMAN SUPPLIES. NASHVILLE. TENNESSEE. PRINTED IN U.S.A.

should then be transferred to the Dismissed Member
file.

When corrections need to be made in any church
or organization records, the Record Correction form
is available. Requests for changes such as married
name, address, or telephone can be requested by fill-
ing out the Record Correction form and sending to
the proper church officer or church secretary.

The Member's Record of Training and Service is
designed to maintain a current account of a member's
record of completed training and service. This record
is in the form of a 9½ by 11 file folder. Church study
course and other training may be recorded on the file
folder in the appropriate space. Individual diplomas,
certificates, and seals that have been earned for specific training can be kept inside the file folder. (See
page 138.)

RECORD CORRECTION
Form 4

☐ Sunday School
☐ Training Union
☐ Church Music

Name	Department	Class/group/choir/etc.

Drop Request	☐ Attending another church	Other reason	
	☐ Moved	Information source	
	☐ Died		

Transfer Request	Transfer to: Class/group/choir/etc.	Department
	Reason for transfer	

Information Changes	New address	New home phone no.
	Other new or changed information	

Signatures	Correction requested by	Title	Date
	Correction approved by	Title	Date

Code 4380-04, Broadman Supplies, Nashville, Tenn., Printed in U.S.A.

MEMBER'S RECORD OF TRAINING AND SERVICE

Name _____

Record of Service in Church Organizations
(Sunday School; Church Training; Music; Women Missionary Union; Brotherhood; Committees; Officers)

Organization	Office Held	Date

Attendance at Assemblies, Conventions, and Conferences
(Glorieta; Ridgecrest; State; Association; Etc.)

Date	Meeting Attended

Church Financial Records

Adequate church financial records assist greatly in developing persons as good stewards. When accurate financial records are maintained, a church can secure information required for planning an annual program of stewardship development. Financial records are also essential if church monies are to be spent according to plan.

The following church financial records are available from Baptist Book Stores.

Stewardship Commitment Card

Church Member?_____ S. S. Member?_____ Card No._____

NAME:

ADDRESS: PHONE:

DEPT.:   CLASS:

Recognizing my personal responsibility as a steward of God, and demonstrating my faith in him I make the following commitment:

☐ I am a tither: I will now step up from God's minimum to _____% and estimate my gifts to average $ _____ per week.

☐ I will tithe and estimate my gifts to be $_____ per week.

☐ Although I am not yet a tither, I will give a definite amount for the coming year and estimate my gifts to be $_____ per week.

Signed _____

(This may be increased, decreased, or cancelled at any time by notifying the treasurer.)
Code 4385-36, SR-496, Broadman Supplies, Nashville, Tenn. Printed in USA

Stewardship Commitment Card
"Moreover it is required in stewards that a man be found faithful." I Cor. 4:2

Individual Report Envelope

INDIVIDUAL REPORT ENVELOPE

Name _____ Sunday _____

If VISITOR Give

Home Address _____

Class _____ Amount of Offering $ _____

Check (✓) each point attained and add up total grade.

Attendance 20%	On Time 10%	Bible Brought 10%	Offering 10%	Prepared Lesson 30%	Preaching Attendance 20%	Total Grade

Visits Made	Phone Calls	Letters & Cards	Total Contacts

Form 15 Broadman Supplies

Offering Envelope

MY REGULAR OFFERING FOR THE UNIFIED BUDGET OF MY CHURCH

NAME ....

AMOUNT $..........

CLASS .... DEPT. ....

- [ ] Present
- [ ] Bible Brought
- [ ] Bible Read Daily
- [ ] Lesson Studied
- [ ] Giving

- [ ] Worship Attendance
- [ ] Outreach:
  - Visits to Prospects_____
  - Other Contacts with Prospects_____

- [ ] Ministry:
  - Ministry Actions to Members_____
  - Ministry Actions to Others_____

Code 4336-13   BROADMAN SUPPLIES, Nashville, Tennessee   Printed in U.S.A.

Summary of Receipts

SECTION I — CASH ITEMS

RECEIPT	SUNDAY SCHOOL	MORNING WORSHIP	EVENING WORSHIP	Sunday RECEIVED DURING WEEK	TOTAL
CHECKS					
CURRENCY					
COINS					
TOTAL					

SECTION II — SOURCES OF CASH

BUDGET — ENVELOPE		
BUDGET — LOOSE PLATE		
DESIGNATED		
MISC.		
TOTAL*		
DIFFERENCE		
TOTAL DEPOSIT		
CERTIFIED CORRECT BY**		

*SHOULD AGREE WITH TOTAL IN SECTION I; IF IT DOES NOT, ENTER DIFFERENCE ON NEXT LINE.

**SHOULD BE INITIALED BY AT LEAST TWO MEMBERS OF THE COUNTING COMMITTEE.

Purchase Requisition

PURCHASE REQUISITION

Date of Requisition	Date Needed	Budget Code		Using Department		
May be Purchased From	(Name)	(Street Address)	(City)	(State)	(Zip Code)	

QUANTITY	ITEM NO., DESCRIPTION, SIZE	Unit Price	AMOUNT

Requisitioned By	Purchase Authorized By	Received By	Date

4585-18 Broadman Supplies, Nashville, Tennessee. Printed in U.S.A.

PURCHASE ORDER

CHURCH .
NAME AND .
ADDRESS .

ORDER NO _____
Please Refer To This Number
On Your Invoice Labels, and
Correspondence.

ORDERED .
FROM .

DATE ORDERED	SHIP VIA	DELIVER ORDER BY	BUDGET CODE	ACCT. NO.	TERMS
QUANTITY	DESCRIPTION			UNIT PRICE	AMOUNT

CODE 4585-18 BROADMAN SUPPLIES, NASHVILLE, TENN. PRINTED IN U.S.A.

AUTHORIZED SIGNATURE

Record of Contribution

RECORD OF CONTRIBUTIONS

CHURCH FINANCE RECORD SYSTEM

Your church appreciates your tithes and offerings.
Please compare with your records and report any errors.

Envelope No.

Year Beginning

Budget Pledge

$ Per Week

Sun-day	First Quarter		Second Quarter		Third Quarter		Fourth Quarter		Date	Special Gifts	Amount	
1												
2												
3												
4												
5												
1												
2												
3												
4												
5												
1												
2												
3												
4												
5												
Paid this Quarter	/////											
Paid To Date												
Pledge To Date									*Total Specials for Year			
Over Pledge									Total Budget for Year			
Under Pledge									Total Budget and Specials For Year			

* Totals for special gifts shown only at end of year.   Keep for Income Tax Purposes

4J85-11 CF-11 BROADMAN SUPPLIES, NASHVILLE, TENN. PTD. IN U. S. A

Church Financial Guidelines

1. A church should depend on the gifts of its member as the primary financial support.

2. A church budget should be developed and pledged each year by church members.

3. A stewardship committee should be elected to serve the church in stewardship planning, stewardship promotion, and financial administration.

4. A church should bond each person who handles church money.

5. Envelopes should be provided each person who contributes to support the church program.

6. One person should be selected to serve as purchasing agent.

7. One person should be selected to serve as disbursing agent.

8. All checks will be signed and countersigned by different persons authorized by the church.

9. A record of contribution should be maintained on all contributions and reported quarterly to contributors.

10. All church financial records should be audited annually by church-authorized individuals not involved in regular church financial matters.

11. A report on all church finances should be made monthly to the church.

14. RELATIONSHIPS
Church, Association, State Convention,
Southern Baptist Convention

Baptists believe that the Scriptures provide direction for maintaining proper relationships between the church and other bodies of the denomination. Paul encouraged the early Christians to follow the Scriptures as their spiritual foundation. "All scripture is given by inspiration of God, and is profitable for doctrine, for reproof, for correction, for instruction in righteousness: that the man of God may be perfect, thoroughly furnished unto all good works" (2 Tim. 3:16–17).

Ten New Testament principles of polity are cited by Lee H. McCoy in *Understanding Baptist Polity* published by Convention Press. An awareness of these principles will help in understanding why Baptists follow a congregational type of polity. Adherence to these principles also will help persons understand why Baptists prefer a less efficient approach to relationships in order to remain true to principles set forth in the Bible.

Ten New Testament Principles on Polity

1. God is the sovereign ruler of all mankind.
2. Christ is the head and divine teacher of the church.

3. The Holy Spirit is our guide and source of power.
4. The Bible is the supreme authority of the church.
5. Each individual is competent and free under God.
6. Each church is an autonomous, spiritual democracy.
7. A church is a regenerate body.
8. Church members have equal rights and privileges.
9. Church cooperation is a voluntary matter.
10. Religious liberty is an inalienable right.

Principles Shape Relationships

Baptists have forged their concepts of congregational polity from their understanding of the Bible, which they see as the supreme authority for the church. With Christ as the head of the church, there is no place for a bishop or for decreasing levels of authority.

If each individual is competent and free under God, then church members should be free to make decisions they think are right under the leadership of God. When each church is considered an autonomous, spiritual democracy, there must be strong opposition to any type of control. Baptists hold firmly to the belief that each member of the congregation has an inalienable right to voice his viewpoint under the leadership of the Holy Spirit.

One church has no authority over another church just as no pastor or member has authority over the church. Each member has equal rights and privileges. Each church has the right of decision regarding how or with whom it will cooperate.

Equality and autonomy bring responsibility. Neither individuals nor churches can live in isolation. There are relationships that strengthen and bring renewal. Such strengthening relationships, therefore, grow in an atmosphere of mutual interdependence as they fellowship together in associations, state Baptist conventions, and the Southern Baptist Convention. Various Baptist bodies working together by voluntary desire bring unique and productive achievements without usurping the autonomy or authority of any one body. One of the noblest attainments of man is his ability to relate to another person or group of persons without sacrificing his own integrity or selfhood.

Relationships Between Church and Denominational Bodies

Churches are the basic units in Baptist work. Churches are of divine origin and are foundational to all that is accomplished. From the churches come the elected "messengers" to attend meetings of the association, state Baptist convention, and Southern Baptist Convention. Churches furnish the financial and leadership resources by which extensive work can be carried out by denominational bodies.

As singular bodies under the lordship of Christ, churches are not a part of a master Baptist church. Neither is it correct to infer that a church is a member church of a state Baptist convention or the Southern Baptist Convention.

An overview of Baptist work shows four unique bodies. First, there are churches. These are primary and foundational. Second, there are three other bodies that are all similar but different. They are the association, state Baptist convention, and Southern Baptist Convention. Each of the three denominational bodies is uniquely autonomous but interdependent in a fellowship of Baptists.

As a church is made up of baptized Christian believers, each of the three denominational bodies is comprised of selected individuals from the churches. Churches elect messengers to attend the annual associational meeting. These persons are not delegates in that their churches do not delegate authority to them. These messengers do not speak for their church but only for themselves as they are led by the Holy Spirit.

Churches do not comprise the membership of an association. Associations do not comprise the membership of a state Baptist convention. And state Baptist conventions do not make up the membership of the Southern Baptist Convention. To each of these denominational bodies in regular session churches send messengers to vote as individuals. Upon their return to their church, these members should be given opportunity to report on the events that took place and to bring encouragement to fellow Christians regarding the work being achieved cooperatively.

Denominational bodies, on the other hand, are not required to accept the messengers who are sent by churches. Each association, state Baptist convention, and Southern Baptist Convention decides whom it will accept. Each denominational body provides a committee to examine the credentials of the messengers attending the annual meeting. Fellowship with messengers is sometimes withdrawn or not extended if established qualifications for affiliation are not adequate.

Another unique quality of the church and the three denominational bodies is that no person or group can overide decisions that each makes. There is no hierarchial structure for appeal. Each body can change its former decision, but no outside authority can force a change in decision.

Baptist polity admittedly does not provide the highest qualities of efficiency, but Baptists have been willing to lose some efficiency in order to remain close to principles of polity found in the Bible.